At Issue

| Technology and
| the Cloud

Other Books in the At Issue Series:

At Issue

Technology and the Cloud

David Haugen and Susan Musser, Book Editors

GREENHAVEN PRESS
A part of Gale, Cengage Learning

GALE
CENGAGE Learning·

Detroit • New York • San Francisco • New Haven, Conn • Waterville, Maine • London

Elizabeth Des Chenes, *Director, Publishing Solutions*

For more information, contact:
Greenhaven Press
27500 Drake Rd.
Farmington Hills, MI 48331-3535
Or you can visit our Internet site at gale.cengage.com

For product information and technology assistance, contact us at

Gale Customer Support, 1-800-877-4253
For permission to use material from this text or product, submit all requests online at www.cengage.com/permissions.

Further permissions questions can be e-mailed to permissionrequest@cengage.com.

Articles in Greenhaven Press anthologies are often edited for length to meet page requirements. In addition, original titles of these works are changed to clearly present the main thesis and to explicitly indicate the author's opinion. Every effort is made to ensure that Greenhaven Press accurately reflects the original intent of the authors. Every effort has been made to trace the owners of copyrighted material.

Cover photograph reproduced with permission of Brand X Pictures.

LIBRARY OF CONGRESS CATALOGING-IN-PUBLICATION DATA

Technology and the cloud / David Haugen and Susan Musser, book editors.
   p. cm. -- (At issue)
Includes bibliographical references and index.
ISBN 978-0-7377-6207-5 (hardcover) -- ISBN 978-0-7377-6208-2 (pbk.)
1. Cloud computing. I. Haugen, David M., 1969- II. Musser, Susan.
QA76.585.T43 2012
004.67'82--dc23

2012023325

Printed in the United States of America
1 2 3 4 5 6 7 16 15 14 13 12

Contents

Introduction

Cloud computing is now common among many information technology (IT) providers and consumers, yet the notion of cloud computing remains confusing to many—even to those who routinely take advantage of cloud services. One challenge to understanding cloud computing stems from the term itself. The "cloud" in cloud computing is neither a physical location nor a specific technology; it is a service model or an approach to uniting sellers and consumers through services provided over the Internet. Because the interface between the provider and user is virtual, the cloud analogy may seem apt. For example, cloud storage services typically provide users with a portion of a computer server that exists in a location unknown to the user, but the user can draw on that storage at any time from a computer terminal of his or her choice. Sometimes the storage space is spread across multiple linked servers that reside in numerous locations across the globe, enhancing the concept of a nebulous cloud of networked virtual spaces. However, an important facet of cloud computing is that, even though the storage may exist "out there" in that virtual network, the user can access stored data instantaneously, making an immediate bridge between service and consumption. This same model can be applied to vendors who provide applications, on-demand services, or computational power rather than just data storage. For instance, a seller might provide a software program that can be accessed by users and opened as an application on a personal computer. The program does not exist on the user's computer; its functions are simply opened and utilized and then closed whenever the user desires.

In an April 7, 2008, article, Eric Knorr, the editor-in-chief of InfoWorld, an online resource on emerging technologies, tries to demystify the vagueness of the term by stating, "Cloud computing comes into focus only when you think about what IT always needs: a way to increase capacity or add capabilities on the fly without investing in new infrastructure, training new personnel, or licensing new software. Cloud computing encompasses any subscription-based or pay-per-use service that, in real time over the Internet, extends IT's existing capabilities." Extending a pay-per-use service in real time means that providers have to guarantee that their programs will be accessible on demand, often compelling providers to tap resources from multiple servers so that no "downtime" hampers business. While some providers offer specific software packages to consumers over the Internet, one unique avenue of cloud computing permits users to pick and choose parts of software and services that they specifically need and thus customize their own suite of programs. In addition, users can simply drop in new programs or delete no-longer-needed packages with ease. This, as Knorr writes, gives vendors a way of fulfilling consumers' needs without acquiring new personnel or greatly expanding infrastructure.

While cloud computing seems to offer advantages to both providers and consumers, many observers and clients have voiced concerns about the safety of information manipulated over virtual networks. In a March 12, 2010, brief for CNN.com, Lara Farrar stated that "a recent study from *CIO Magazine* found that despite the increasing popularity of outsourced computing, 50 percent of CEOs surveyed said safety was one of their biggest worries." As Farrar recounts, some of those concerned leaders worry that servers could crash and potentially delete data; others are hesitant to send sensitive data offsite (into the virtual world) where users must relinquish the in-house security measures they trust and subsequently place faith in the service provider's protections over which users have no control. Farrar continues, "Such high concentrations of information also create the perfect storm for hacking."

Although such threats exist, some commentators are convinced that the risks are no greater than they have always been for any type of computing. In a May 24, 2011, snippet on the website for Kexino, a business consulting company, Gee Ranasinha writes, "Yes, cloud computing-based systems are fallible—in the same way that any computing system is regardless of where it's based." Ranasinha maintains that much of the fear comes from a few headline-grabbing security breaches or errors that happen to big-name giants and that this focus ignores the thousands of companies that utilize the cloud safely every business day. Still, questions and concerns persist as the trend toward cloud computing gains momentum in commerce, government, education, and private sectors.

Some viewpoints in *At Issue: Technology and the Cloud* address the controversies surrounding security of this burgeoning virtual marketplace. Other viewpoints in the volume debate the uses and efficiency of the cloud. While some viewpoint authors conceive of the cloud as a truly liberating aspect of the World Wide Web, bringing together remote services and customers and meeting the demands of a highly globalized society, other authors maintain that this new frontier poses many problems that run the gamut from infringing on property rights to creating adverse environmental impacts. Collectively, the viewpoints in this anthology suggest that cloud computing, like all new applications of technology, must find a way to satisfy user demands while promoting safety and cost effectiveness.

1

Cloud Computing: An Overview

William Voorsluys, James Broberg, and Rajkumar Buyya

William Voorsluys is a graduate student in computer science and James Broberg is a postdoctoral fellow, both at the University of Melbourne in Australia. Rajkumar Buyya is a professor of computer science at the same institution. Buyya and Broberg served as editors of the book Cloud Computing: Principles and Paradigms.

The definition of cloud computing can be fairly elastic. In its most restrictive sense, though, cloud computing refers to a network relationship in which computing infrastructure (whether storage, processing, or applications) exists on remote servers accessed through the Internet. The most common model entails clients paying for provider services hosted on those servers yet manipulated on the client's computer. This system allows users to relinquish hardware and software requirements and take advantage of virtual computing at a relatively low cost.

When plugging an electric appliance into an outlet, we care neither how electric power is generated nor how it gets to that outlet. This is possible because electricity is virtualized; that is, it is readily available from a wall socket that hides power generation stations and a huge distribution grid. When extended to information technologies, this concept means delivering useful functions while hiding how their internals work. Computing itself, to be considered fully virtualized, must allow computers to be built from distributed components such as processing, storage, data, and software resources.

Technologies such as *cluster, grid*, and now, *cloud* computing, have all aimed at allowing access to large amounts of computing power in a fully virtualized manner, by aggregating resources and offering a single system view. In addition, an important aim of these technologies has been delivering computing as a utility. Utility computing describes a business model for on-demand delivery of computing power; consumers pay providers based on usage ("pay-as-you-go"), similar to the way in which we currently obtain services from traditional public utility services such as water, electricity, gas, and telephony.

The Cloud: Computing Service on Demand

Cloud computing has been coined as an umbrella term to describe a category of sophisticated on-demand computing services initially offered by commercial providers, such as Amazon, Google, and Microsoft. It denotes a model on which a computing infrastructure is viewed as a "cloud," from which businesses and individuals access applications from anywhere in the world on demand. The main principle behind this model is offering computing, storage, and software "as a service."

Many practitioners in the commercial and academic spheres have attempted to define exactly what "cloud computing" is and what unique characteristics it presents. [In a 2009 article for *Future Generation Computer Systems*, Rajkumar] Buyya et al. have defined it as follows: "Cloud is a parallel and distributed computing system consisting of a collection of inter-connected and virtualised computers that are dynamically provisioned and presented as one or more unified computing resources based on service-level agreements (SLA) established through negotiation between the service provider and consumers."

[In a 2009 article for *SIGCOMM Computer Communications Review*, Luis] Vaquero et al. have stated "clouds are a large pool of easily usable and accessible virtualized resources (such as hardware, development platforms and/or services). These resources can be dynamically reconfigured to adjust to a variable load (scale), allowing also for an optimum resource utilization. This pool of resources is typically exploited by a pay-per-use model in which guarantees are offered by the Infrastructure Provider by means of customized Service Level Agreements."

A recent [2009] McKinsey and Co. report claims that "Clouds are hardware-based services offering compute, network, and storage capacity where: Hardware management is highly abstracted from the buyer, buyers incur infrastructure costs as variable OPEX [operational expenditures], and infrastructure capacity is highly elastic."

A cloud should have: (i) pay-per-use (no ongoing commitment, utility prices); (ii) elastic capacity and the illusion of infinite resources; (iii) self-service interface; and (iv) resources that are abstracted or virtualised.

A [2009] report from the University of California Berkeley summarized the key characteristics of cloud computing as: "(1) the illusion of infinite computing resources; (2) the elimination of an up-front commitment by cloud users; and (3) the ability to pay for use . . . as needed . . ."

The National Institute of Standards and Technology (NIST) characterizes cloud computing as ". . . a pay-per-use model for enabling available, convenient, on-demand network access to a shared pool of configurable computing resources (e.g. networks, servers, storage, applications, services) that can be rapidly provisioned and released with minimal management effort or service provider interaction." . . .

While there are countless other definitions, there seems to be common characteristics between the most notable ones listed above, which a cloud should have: (i) pay-per-use (no ongoing commitment, utility prices); (ii) elastic capacity and the illusion of infinite resources; (iii) self-service interface; and (iv) resources that are abstracted or virtualised.

Consumers can attain reduction on IT-related costs by choosing to obtain cheaper services from external providers as opposed to heavily investing on IT infrastructure and personnel hiring.

In addition to raw computing and storage, cloud computing providers usually offer a broad range of software services. They also include APIs [application programming interface] and development tools that allow developers to build seamlessly scalable applications upon their services. The ultimate goal is allowing customers to run their everyday IT [information technology] infrastructure "in the cloud."

A lot of hype has surrounded the cloud computing area in its infancy, often considered the most significant switch in the IT world since the advent of the Internet. In midst of such hype, a great deal of confusion arises when trying to define what cloud computing is and which computing infrastructures can be termed as "clouds." . . .

From On-site to Remote Service Providers

We are currently experiencing a switch in the IT world, from in-house generated computing power into utility-supplied computing resources delivered over the Internet as Web services. This trend is similar to what occurred about a century ago when factories, which used to generate their own electric power, realized that it was cheaper just plugging their machines into the newly formed electric power grid.

Computing delivered as a utility can be defined as "on demand delivery of infrastructure, applications, and business processes in a security-rich, shared, scalable, and based computer environment over the Internet for a fee" [according to Michael Rappa in a 2004 issue of *IBM Systems Journal*]. This model brings benefits to both consumers and providers of IT services. Consumers can attain reduction on IT-related costs by choosing to obtain cheaper services from external providers as opposed to heavily investing on IT infrastructure and personnel hiring. The "on-demand" component of this model allows consumers to adapt their IT usage to rapidly increasing or unpredictable computing needs.

Providers of IT services achieve better operational costs; hardware and software infrastructures are built to provide multiple solutions and serve many users, thus increasing efficiency and ultimately leading to faster return on investment (ROI) as well as lower total cost of ownership (TCO).

Several technologies have in some way aimed at turning the utility computing concept into reality. In the 1970s, companies who offered common data processing tasks, such as payroll automation, operated time-shared mainframes as utilities, which could serve dozens of applications and often operated close to 100% of their capacity. In fact, mainframes had to operate at very high utilization rates simply because they were very expensive and costs should be justified by efficient usage.

The mainframe era collapsed with the advent of fast and inexpensive microprocessors and IT data centers moved to collections of commodity servers. Apart from its clear advantages, this new model inevitably led to isolation of workload into dedicated servers, mainly due to incompatibilities between software stacks and operating systems. In addition, the unavailability of efficient computer networks meant that IT infrastructure should be hosted in proximity to where it would be consumed. Altogether, these facts have prevented the utility computing reality of taking place on modern computer systems.

Similar to old electricity generation stations, which used to power individual factories, computing servers and desktop computers in a modern organization are often underutilized, since IT infrastructure is configured to handle theoretical demand peaks. In addition, in the early stages of electricity generation, electric current could not travel long distances without significant voltage losses. However, new paradigms emerged culminating on transmission systems able to make electricity available hundreds of kilometers far off from where it is generated. Likewise, the advent of increasingly fast fiber-optics networks has relit the fire, and new technologies for enabling sharing of computing power over great distances have appeared.

Cloud computing services are usually backed by large-scale data centers composed of thousands of computers.

These facts reveal the potential of delivering computing services with the speed and reliability that businesses enjoy with their local machines. The benefits of economies of scale and high utilization allow providers to offer computing services for a fraction of what it costs for a typical company that generates its own computing power. . . .

Hardware Virtualization

Cloud computing services are usually backed by large-scale data centers composed of thousands of computers. Such data centers are built to serve many users and host many disparate applications. For this purpose, hardware virtualization can be considered as a perfect fit to overcome most operational issues of data center building and maintenance.

The idea of virtualizing a computer system's resources, including processors, memory, and I/O [input/output] devices, has been well established for decades, aiming at improving sharing and utilization of computer systems. Hardware virtualization allows running multiple operating systems [OS] and software stacks on a single physical platform. A software layer, the virtual machine monitor (VMM), also called a hypervisor, mediates access to the physical hardware presenting to each guest operating system a virtual machine (VM), which is a set of virtual platform interfaces.

The advent of several innovative technologies—multi-core chips, paravirtualization, hardware-assisted virtualization, and live migration of VMs—has contributed to an increasing adoption of virtualization on server systems. Traditionally, perceived benefits were improvements on sharing and utilization, better manageability, and higher reliability. More recently, with the adoption of virtualization on a broad range of server and client systems, researchers and practitioners have been emphasizing three basic capabilities regarding management of workload in a virtualized system, namely isolation, consolidation, and migration.

Workload isolation is achieved since all program instructions are fully confined inside a VM, which leads to improvements in security. Better reliability is also achieved because software failures inside one VM do not affect others. Moreover, better performance control is attained since execution of one VM should not affect the performance of another VM.

The consolidation of several individual and heterogeneous workloads onto a single physical platform leads to better system utilization. This practice is also employed for overcoming potential software and hardware incompatibilities in case of upgrades, given that it is possible to run legacy and new operation systems concurrently.

Workload migration, also referred to as application mobility, targets at facilitating hardware maintenance, load balancing, and disaster recovery. It is done by encapsulating a guest OS state within a VM and allowing it to be suspended, fully serialized, migrated to a different platform, and resumed immediately or preserved to be restored at a later date. A VM's state includes a full disk or partition image, configuration files, and an image of its RAM [random access memory]. . . .

Layers and Types of Clouds

Cloud computing services are divided into three classes, according to the abstraction level of the capability provided and the service model of providers, namely: (1) Infrastructure as a Service, (2) Platform as a Service, and (3) Software as a Service.

Traditional desktop applications such as word processing and spreadsheet can now be accessed as a service in the Web.

These abstraction levels can also be viewed as a layered architecture where services of a higher layer can be composed from services of the underlying layer. . . . A core middleware manages physical resources and the VMs deployed on top of them; in addition, it provides the required features (e.g., accounting and billing) to offer multi-tenant pay-as-you-go services. Cloud development environments are built on top of infrastructure services to offer application development and deployment capabilities; in this level, various programming models, libraries, APIs, and mashup editors enable the creation of a range of business, Web, and scientific applications. Once deployed in the cloud, these applications can be consumed by end users.

Infrastructure as a Service. Offering virtualized resources (computation, storage, and communication) on demand is known as Infrastructure as a Service (IaaS). A *cloud infrastruc-*

ture enables on-demand provisioning of servers running several choices of operating systems and a customized software stack. Infrastructure services are considered to be the bottom layer of cloud computing systems. . . .

Platform as a Service. In addition to infrastructure-oriented clouds that provide raw computing and storage services, another approach is to offer a higher level of abstraction to make a cloud easily programmable, known as Platform as a Service (PaaS). A *cloud platform* offers an environment on which developers create and deploy applications and do not necessarily need to know how many processors or how much memory that applications will be using. In addition, multiple programming models and specialized services (e.g., data access, authentication, and payments) are offered as building blocks to new applications. . . .

Consumers of cloud computing services expect on-demand, nearly instant access to resources.

Software as a Service. Applications reside on the top of the cloud stack. Services provided by this layer can be accessed by end users through Web portals. Therefore, consumers are increasingly shifting from locally installed computer programs to on-line software services that offer the same functionally. Traditional desktop applications such as word processing and spreadsheet can now be accessed as a service in the Web. This model of delivering applications, known as Software as a Service (SaaS), alleviates the burden of software maintenance for customers and simplifies development and testing for providers.

Expected Features of a Cloud

Certain features of a cloud are essential to enable services that truly represent the cloud computing model and satisfy expectations of consumers, and cloud offerings must be (i) self-service, (ii) per-usage metered and billed, (iii) elastic, and (iv) customizable.

Self-Service. Consumers of cloud computing services expect on-demand, nearly instant access to resources. To support this expectation, clouds must allow self-service access so that customers can request, customize, pay, and use services without intervention of human operators.

Per-Usage Metering and Billing. Cloud computing eliminates up-front commitment by users, allowing them to request and use only the necessary amount. Services must be priced on a short-term basis (e.g., by the hour), allowing users to release (and not pay for) resources as soon as they are not needed. For these reasons, clouds must implement features to allow efficient trading of service such as pricing, accounting, and billing. Metering should be done accordingly for different types of service (e.g., storage, processing, and bandwidth) and usage promptly reported, thus providing greater transparency.

Elasticity. Cloud computing gives the illusion of infinite computing resources available on demand. Therefore users expect clouds to rapidly provide resources in any quantity at any time. In particular, it is expected that the additional resources can be (a) provisioned, possibly automatically, when an application load increases and (b) released when load decreases (scale up and down).

Customization. In a multi-tenant cloud a great disparity between user needs is often the case. Thus, resources rented from the cloud must be highly customizable. In the case of infrastructure services, customization means allowing users to deploy specialized virtual appliances and to be given privileged (root) access to the virtual servers. Other service classes (PaaS and SaaS) offer less flexibility and are not suitable for general-purpose computing, but still are expected to provide a certain level of customization.

2

Cloud Computing Threatens User Freedom and Should Be Avoided

Richard M. Stallman

A computer programmer, Richard M. Stallman founded the GNU Project, a collective that has been creating and distributing a free operating system for computers since 1983. He also is the founder of the Free Software Foundation, which fights against digital property rights so that software may be used and modified to help society.

The vague term "cloud computing" masks the fact that users may not be in control of their data when it is channeled through distant servers. Many Internet applications are set up under software as a service (SaaS) contracts in which users partake of these programs to achieve some end such as photo editing or social networking. However, some of these programs collect user information and utilize it for other purposes such as marketing and generating user profiles. To keep their data private, users should refrain from employing SaaS applications and utilize freeware programs that allow users to control and manipulate their information on their own computers.

On the Internet, proprietary software isn't the only way to lose your freedom. Software as a Service is another way to let someone else have power over your computing.

Background: How Proprietary Software Takes Away Your Freedom

Digital technology can give you freedom; it can also take your freedom away. The first threat to our control over our computing came from proprietary software: software that the users cannot control because the owner (a company such as Apple or Microsoft) controls it. The owner often takes advantage of this unjust power by inserting malicious features such as spyware, back doors, and Digital Restrictions Management (DRM) (referred to as "Digital Rights Management" in their propaganda).

Our solution to this problem is developing free software and rejecting proprietary software. Free software means that you, as a user, have four essential freedoms:

- to run the program as you wish

- to study and change the source code so it does what you wish

- to redistribute exact copies

- to redistribute copies of your modified versions

With free software, we, the users, take back control of our computing. Proprietary software still exists, but we can exclude it from our lives and many of us have done so. However, we now face a new threat to our control over our computing: Software as a Service. For our freedom's sake, we have to reject that too.

How Software as a Service Takes Away Your Freedom

Software as a Service (SaaS) means that someone sets up a network server that does certain computing tasks—running spreadsheets, word processing, translating text into another language, etc.—then invites users to do their computing on that server. Users send their data to the server, which does

their computing on the data thus provided, then sends the results back or acts on them directly.

These servers wrest control from the users even more in-
exorably than proprietary software. With proprietary software,
users typically get an executable file but not the source code.
That makes it hard for programmers to study the code that is
running, so it's hard to determine what the program really
does, and hard to change it.

With SaaS, the users do not have even the executable file:
it is on the server, where the users can't see or touch it. Thus
it is impossible for them to ascertain what it really does, and
impossible to change it.

Furthermore, SaaS automatically leads to harmful consequences equivalent to the malicious features of certain proprietary software. For instance, some proprietary programs are
"spyware": the program sends out data about users' computing activities. Microsoft Windows sends information about
users' activities to Microsoft. Windows Media Player and Real-
Player report what each user watches or listens to.

---

*SaaS is equivalent to total spyware and a gaping wide
back door, and gives the server operator unjust power
over the user.*

Unlike proprietary software, SaaS does not require covert
code to obtain the user's data. Instead, users must send their
data to the server in order to use it. This has the same effect
as spyware: the server operator gets the data. He gets it with
no special effort, by the nature of SaaS.

Some proprietary programs can mistreat users under remote command. For instance, Windows has a back door with
which Microsoft can forcibly change any software on the machine. The Amazon Kindle e-book reader (whose name suggests it's intended to burn people's books) has an Orwellian
back door that Amazon used in 2009 to remotely delete Kindle

copies of Orwell's books *1984* and *Animal Farm* which the users had purchased from Amazon.

SaaS inherently gives the server operator the power to change the software in use, or the users' data being operated on. Once again, no special code is needed to do this.

Thus, SaaS is equivalent to total spyware and a gaping wide back door, and gives the server operator unjust power over the user. We can't accept that.

Untangling the SaaS Issue from the Proprietary Software Issue

SaaS and proprietary software lead to similar harmful results, but the causal mechanisms are different. With proprietary software, the cause is that you have and use a copy which is difficult or illegal to change. With SaaS, the cause is that you use a copy you don't have.

These two issues are often confused, and not only by accident. Web developers use the vague term "web application" to lump the server software together with programs run on your machine in your browser. Some web pages install nontrivial or even large JavaScript programs temporarily into your browser without informing you. When these JavaScript programs are nonfree, they are as bad as any other nonfree software. Here, however, we are concerned with the problem of the server software itself.

> *The original purpose of web servers wasn't to do computing for you, it was to publish information for you to access.*

Many free software supporters assume that the problem of SaaS will be solved by developing free software for servers. For the server operator's sake, the programs on the server had better be free; if they are proprietary, their owners have power over the server. That's unfair to the operator, and doesn't help you at all. But if the programs on the server are free, that doesn't protect you as the server's user from the effects of SaaS. They give freedom to the operator, but not to you.

Releasing the server software source code does benefit the community: suitably skilled users can set up similar servers, perhaps changing the software. But none of these servers would give you control over computing you do on it, unless it's *your* server. The rest would all be SaaS. SaaS always subjects you to the power of the server operator, and the only remedy is, *Don't use SaaS!* Don't use someone else's server to do your own computing on data provided by you.

Distinguishing SaaS from Other Network Services

Does avoiding SaaS mean you refuse to use any network servers run by anyone other than you? Not at all. Most servers do not raise this issue, because the job you do with them isn't your own computing except in a trivial sense.

The original purpose of web servers wasn't to do computing for you, it was to publish information for you to access. Even today this is what most web sites do, and it doesn't pose the SaaS problem, because accessing someone's published information isn't a matter of doing your own computing. Neither is publishing your own materials via a blog site or a microblogging service such as Twitter or identi.ca. The same goes for communication not meant to be private, such as chat groups. Social networking can extend into SaaS; however, at root it is just a method of communication and publication, not SaaS. If you use the service for minor editing of what you're going to communicate, that is not a significant issue.

Services such as search engines collect data from around the web and let you examine it. Looking through their collection of data isn't your own computing in the usual sense— you didn't provide that collection—so using such a service to search the web is not SaaS. (However, using someone else's search engine to implement a search facility for your own site *is* SaaS.)

E-commerce is not SaaS, because the computing isn't solely yours; rather, it is done jointly for you and another party. So there's no particular reason why you alone should expect to control that computing. The real issue in e-commerce is whether you trust the other party with your money and personal information.

Using a joint project's servers isn't SaaS because the computing you do in this way isn't yours personally. For instance, if you edit pages on Wikipedia, you are not doing your own computing; rather, you are collaborating in Wikipedia's computing.

Wikipedia controls its own servers, but groups can face the problem of SaaS if they do their group activities on someone else's server. Fortunately, development hosting sites such as Savannah and SourceForge don't pose the SaaS problem, because what groups do there is mainly publication and public communication, rather than their own private computing.

Some sites offer multiple services, and if one is not SaaS, another may be SaaS.

Multiplayer games are a group activity carried out on someone else's server, which makes them SaaS. But where the data involved is just the state of play and the score, the worst wrong the operator might commit is favoritism. You might well ignore that risk, since it seems unlikely and very little is at stake. On the other hand, when the game becomes more than just a game, the issue changes.

Which online services are SaaS? Google Docs is a clear example. Its basic activity is editing, and Google encourages people to use it for their own editing; this is SaaS. It offers the added feature of collaborative editing, but adding participants doesn't alter the fact that editing on the server is SaaS. (In addition, Google Docs is unacceptable because it installs a large nonfree JavaScript program into the users' browsers.) If using a service for communication or collaboration requires doing substantial parts of your own computing with it too, that computing is SaaS even if the communication is not.

Some sites offer multiple services, and if one is not SaaS, another may be SaaS. For instance, the main service of Facebook is social networking, and that is not SaaS; however, it supports third-party applications, some of which may be SaaS. Flickr's main service is distributing photos, which is not SaaS, but it also has features for editing photos, which is SaaS.

Some sites whose main service is publication and communication extend it with "contact management": keeping track of people you have relationships with. Sending mail to those people for you is not SaaS, but keeping track of your dealings with them, if substantial, is SaaS.

The real meaning of "cloud computing" is to suggest a devil-may-care approach towards your computing.

If a service is not SaaS, that does not mean it is OK. There are other bad things a service can do. For instance, Facebook distributes video in Flash, which pressures users to run nonfree software, and it gives users a misleading impression of privacy. Those are important issues too, but this article's concern is the issue of SaaS.

The IT [information technology] industry discourages users from considering these distinctions. That's what the buzzword "cloud computing" is for. This term is so nebulous that it could refer to almost any use of the Internet. It includes SaaS and it includes nearly everything else. The term only lends itself to uselessly broad statements.

The real meaning of "cloud computing" is to suggest a devil-may-care approach towards your computing. It says,

"Don't ask questions, just trust every business without hesitation. Don't worry about who controls your computing or who holds your data. Don't check for a hook hidden inside our service before you swallow it." In other words, "Think like a sucker." I prefer to avoid the term.

Dealing with the SaaS Problem

Only a small fraction of all web sites do SaaS; most don't raise the issue. But what should we do about the ones that raise it?

For the simple case, where you are doing your own computing on data in your own hands, the solution is simple: use your own copy of a free software application. Do your text editing with your copy of a free text editor such as GNU Emacs or a free word processor. Do your photo editing with your copy of free software such as GIMP.

Do your work with your own copy of a free program, for your freedom's sake.

But what about collaborating with other individuals? It may be hard to do this at present without using a server. If you use one, don't trust a server run by a company. A mere contract as a customer is no protection unless you could detect a breach and could really sue, and the company probably writes its contracts to permit a broad range of abuses. Police can subpoena your data from the company with less basis than required to subpoena them from you, supposing the company doesn't volunteer them like the US phone companies that illegally wiretapped their customers for [George W.] Bush. If you must use a server, use a server whose operators give you a basis for trust beyond a mere commercial relationship.

However, on a longer time scale, we can create alternatives to using servers. For instance, we can create a peer-to-peer program through which collaborators can share data encrypted. The free software community should develop distributed peer-to-peer replacements for important "web applications". It may be wise to release them under the GNU Affero GP, since they are likely candidates for being converted into server-based programs by someone else. The GNU project is looking for volunteers to work on such replacements. We also invite other free software projects to consider this issue in their design.

In the meantime, if a company invites you to use its server to do your own computing tasks, don't yield; don't use SaaS. Don't buy or install "thin clients", which are simply computers so weak they make you do the real work on a server, unless you're going to use them with *your* server. Use a real computer and keep your data there. Do your work with your own copy of a free program, for your freedom's sake.

3

Cloud Computing Has the Potential to Expand User Freedom

Ryan Paul

Ryan Paul is the editor of Open Ended, *the open source software journal on the Ars Technica website. He also is the creator and lead developer of Gwibber, an open source microblogging client for the GNOME desktop environment.*

The innovations of the open source and free software movements have done much to liberate computer users from reliance on corporate-owned and other proprietary software. There is no reason to believe these same engineers cannot create applications for the Internet that will allow users to take advantage of cloud storage and computing without surrendering control of their data or sacrificing privacy. Those, like Free Software Foundation founder Richard Stallman, who advocate rejecting cloud computing because of its perils are too shortsighted. Open source program designers have already fashioned alternatives to the dominant desktop operating system, and they are hard at work at making cloud computing accessible and secure.

Free Software Foundation founder Richard Stallman [RMS] spent yesterday [September 29, 2008] condemning cloud computing and is calling for users to reject popular web applications. He insists that reliance on web-based software poses a serious risk to freedom and privacy. Cloud computing is just a "hype campaign" perpetrated by software vendors who want to control users, he says, and the only way to fight the problem is to stop using the software.

Cloud computing is one of the most significant emerging trends in the technology industry. Users are becoming increasingly reliant on web applications and remote data storage solutions. The popularity of cloud computing is climbing in both enterprise and consumer markets, and the trend is widely regarded as a game-changing advancement in software deployment and consumption. In light of the growing importance of cloud computing, Stallman's call for its rejection warrants both scrutiny and skepticism.

> *If the software freedom movement is too brittle to withstand the rise of cloud computing, then it's not going to have any serious staying power.*

"It's stupidity. It's worse than stupidity: it's a marketing hype campaign," Stallman told *The Guardian* in reference to cloud computing. "It's just as bad as using a proprietary program. Do your own computing on your own computer with your copy of a freedom-respecting program. If you use a proprietary program or somebody else's web server, you're defenseless. You're putty in the hands of whoever developed that software."

Finding Solutions to the Problems Posed by Cloud Computing

The negative characteristics of cloud computing that Stallman identifies are very real, but the solution that he prescribes seems grossly myopic and counterintuitive. The lack of seamless interoperability between mainstream web applications imposes barriers that limit data portability. Much like proprietary file formats on the desktop, the lack of data portability in closed-web ecosystems creates the potential for vendor lock-in and reduces the amount of control that users have over their own data. Many web applications also have restrictive terms of service that require users to cede some rights to their own data so that it can be exploited by the application providers for invasive advertising or other purposes.

Stallman correctly recognizes those problems, but his belief that the problems are intractable is simply wrong. The open source software movement has found productive ways to address the same kind of problems on the desktop, and I'm confident that reasonable solutions can be found to bring the same level of freedom to the cloud. The challenges posed by new computing paradigms will require the open source software community to evolve and adapt, not collectively stick its head in the sand.

The rapidly shifting landscape in the technology industry demands that participants cultivate a high level of adaptability. Stakeholders have to be willing to keep an open mind and find practical ways to embrace major changes, or risk getting left behind. If the software freedom movement is too brittle to withstand the rise of cloud computing, then it's not going to have any serious staying power.

Experimentation in the Right Direction

Fortunately, I'm not the only open source software enthusiast who doesn't buy into what I view as Stallman's hysteria and defeatism. Earlier this year, tech publisher Tim O'Reilly discussed the issue during a keynote presentation at the annual O'Reilly Open Source Conference (OSCON). O'Reilly acknowledged the challenges posed by cloud computing, but he also pointed out that the vibrant open source software community has already started exploring experimental solutions.

Here at Ars [Technica], we have reported on several intriguing open web service initiatives that have been launched in the past few years. The developers of the open source

GNOME desktop environment, for instance, created the open online.gnome.org web infrastructure so that they could make web integration a core part of the user experience without compromising software freedom. Luis Villa, a law student and GNOME community member, authored a draft for an open services definition last year. His ideas have influenced broad discussion in the GNOME community.

Another really good open web services experiment is Mozilla's Weave synchronization service for Firefox. Weave is still in the early stages of development, but the long-term plan is to provide a secure web storage platform that is accessible to the browser and third-party software components. Weave uses encryption so that the data is never visible to the operator of the server. It also uses the WebDAV protocol and doesn't depend on any specialized server-side capabilities, so it will be easy for users to self-host their Weave storage and use third-party providers for the backend.

The open source Identi.ca microblogging application is another open web service that's gaining users. Identi.ca pioneered the OpenMicroBlogging standard, an interoperability protocol that makes it possible for users to communicate across compatible microblogging services. Identi.ca founder Evan Prodromou is one of many open source community members who is speaking out against Stallman's rejection of cloud computing.

Cloud computing has the potential to expand user freedom in some very important ways.

"I'm very supportive of [Stallman's] concern about cloud computing, and I agree that it's something that the Free Software and Free Culture communities need to address. But in rejecting all network computing, I think RMS has thrown out the baby with the bathwater," Prodromou wrote in a blog entry this morning. "I don't believe loss of absolute control means that you lose your autonomy completely. And I think that exchanging some control in order to participate in social, collaborative computing is ultimately enriching for individuals and for society."

Prodromou is a signatory of the Franklin Street Statement, a roadmap for delivering software freedom in a cloud computing environment. The statement, which was authored by members of the open source software community in collaboration with the Free Software Foundation, encourages service providers to release their software under open licenses and give users the ability to control their own data.

The Cloud Can Bring More Freedom to Users

Another facet of this issue that is worth considering is that cloud computing has the potential to expand user freedom in some very important ways. For instance, the growth of cloud computing and the shift in focus away from the desktop is rapidly eroding the leverage of the companies that control desktop platforms. Microsoft's operating system monopoly, for instance, is largely predicated on the abundance of software that is only available on Windows. If more of that software shifts to the web, users will become less dependent on Windows and will have more freedom to choose which operating system they adopt. That is one of the many factors that has contributed to the recent increase in vendor adoption of Linux on netbook devices.

Stallman's dismissal of cloud computing and call for the categorical rejection of web services is puzzling in light of the potential opportunities created by web technologies and the innovative work that is being done by software freedom advocates to bring openness to the web. Stallman should be using his visibility to promote adoption of the principles embodied in the Franklin Street Statement. Instead he is undermining those efforts by disingenuously dismissing the entire concept of network computing.

4

Hacking Is a Significant Threat to Cloud Computing

Rena Marie Pacella

Rena Marie Pacella is a science writer who works as a contributing editor for Popular Science.

Computer hackers can routinely invade personal computers and networks with ease, and it is much simpler to infiltrate cloud servers. These large conglomerates of linked servers operate by remote access so they forgo firewalls and other protective measures designed to restrict the number of users. Hackers can use this to their advantage, creating fake (or virtual) computers to interact with the servers and feed in malicious viruses that can destroy whole systems or pilfer personal information from them. Engineers are busy creating new means of security to protect this vast array of servers from those who might wish to cause harm.

Last summer [2010] at a DefCon hacking convention in Las Vegas, two security consultants showed a room full of hackers, FBI [Federal Bureau of Investigation] agents and computer-security experts how, with only $6 and a few lines of code, they could knock out a company's website for a full two hours. "Our weapon?" announced David Bryan, a penetration tester at business-security firm Trustwave who goes by the handle VideoMan: "the cloud."

A Collection of Servers

Often breathlessly touted in TV commercials, the cloud is basically an umbrella term for all data that exists beyond the hard drive—everything on the Internet. But to security experts and IT [information technology] professionals, the cloud is actually a collection of multiple, tangible "clouds," remotely accessed server farms that store information, host software, and handle data processing in lieu of household PCs and company servers. Web apps, Internet-run operating systems like Google Chrome, Flickr photos and all the information we post on Facebook live on these servers. Amazon, Microsoft and dozens of other companies offer cloud services that allow anyone with a credit card and an e-mail address to rent pay-as-you-use bandwidth and processing power, and operate "virtual machines" ("virtual" because they are no more than temporarily cordoned-off server space) that they can access from anywhere at any time. Individual and corporate customers can use cloud accounts to host a website, store music or photos, develop apps, or do anything else traditionally done on a desktop or local server.

Numbers on how pervasive cloud hacking might now be are hard to come by, in part because cloud providers often ask their clients to keep attacks quiet.

U.S. businesses will be spending $13 billion annually on cloud services by 2014, up from $3 billion in 2009, according to market-research firm In-Stal. But the cloud's prevalence carries a serious risk: As businesses' operations move to the cloud, all that stored data—everything from personal information to credit-card numbers, as well as businesses' intellectual property—makes for a huge target. And with its easy access to massive computing power and significant gaps in security, the cloud is very hackable. For cybercriminals, the combination of conditions couldn't be more perfect.

Infiltrating the Cloud

"Cloud environments are more vulnerable than regular environments—period," says Rodney Joffe, the senior technologist at telecom giant Neustar. "By their very nature, they assume remote access, unlike regular environments behind a firewall." What's more, they rely on layer upon layer of software to run programs that allocate hardware use, handle customer relations, and perform other functions, as well as all the programs that customers download and install on their virtual machines. Hackers are just starting to dabble in new breeds of malicious code, known as malware, that target weaknesses in cloud software. For example, cybercriminals could create worms that quickly travel through clouds seeking out unpatched holes in the most popular virtual desktops, just as conventional malware exploits vulnerabilities in Microsoft Windows so that it can quickly spread to more users with the same OS [operating system].

"Compromising vulnerable applications in cloud environments is, in most cases, no different from doing so in a traditional network," says Christofer Hoff, the director of cloud solutions at tech conglomerate Cisco Systems. "The issue is that in the cloud, many of the defenses one might rely on elsewhere"—network-based controls such as firewalls—"are not feasible, which makes the exploit easier to execute and harder to detect, and may amplify its impact."

Give a bunch of virtual machines across multiple clouds the same malicious order, and essentially you've created an instant, massive botnet.

Numbers on how pervasive cloud hacking might now be are hard to come by, in part because cloud providers often ask their clients to keep attacks quiet. But if you ask the hackers, as security firm Fortify Software did at DefCon last summer, you get a scary glimpse into the potential depth of cloud-based crime. Twelve percent admitted to attacking the cloud for financial gain—even scarier given that many DefCon hackers are actually hired consultants like Bryan.

Launching Attacks

Today, hackers execute most of their major attacks using large improvised networks, called botnets, which they typically create by infecting websites with viruses that covertly install "backdoors" on visitors' home or office PCs. In this way, a cybercriminal can control hundreds to millions of infected computers, directing them to send out virus-laden spam, clog websites, and troll for holes in legitimate networks to pilfer private information. Botnets won't be replaced as a method of attack—they're too effective and too pervasive. But with the near-limitless processing power and bandwidth available in the cloud, criminals can now easily launch similar attacks from rented or hijacked cloud space, with, Hoff explains, "greater agility, less effort, less exposure and even greater returns."

Attackers have found ways to compromise virtual machines to control traditional PC-based botnets. The next step—if it's not happening already—is virtual-machine, or VM, bots. Give a bunch of virtual machines across multiple clouds the same malicious order, and essentially you've created an instant, massive botnet.

Take Amazon's EC2 cloud, the biggest pay-as-you-use cloud. NASA [National Aeronautics and Space Administration] uses it to analyze mission data. Netflix uses it to stream movies. The DefCon hackers, as they demonstrated in Las Vegas, use it to crash third-party websites. "If we wanted to be bad guys, we could have demanded a hefty ransom from [our target] to halt the attack." Bryan says, "Or we could have sold our services to its competitor."

Bombarding a company's website with bogus traffic is a typical botnet tactic. It's called a distributed denial of service (DDOS), and it's been big cyber-business for a decade. What's new is how easy the cloud makes pulling off a DDOS. Outside the cloud, such attacks require hackers to create a small botnet, which takes a lot of time and code. Instead, Bryan used his e-mail address and credit card to sign up for an Amazon cloud account and then spun up three VMs, which look like standard computer desktops. He and his associate Mike Anderson, an analyst at security firm NetSPI, wrote a program that told each virtual machine to send 10,000 empty data packets to a target site's Web server every second. The scheme wreaked havoc without so much as an e-mail from Amazon, Anderson says. What's more, once he shut down the VMs, there was no trace of the nefarious activity.

A Threat Multiplied Across Virtual Machines

Now imagine if their target had been in a cloud too. The DDOS attack would force the site to consume a huge amount of computing power and cause its operators to rack up enormous and potentially business-killing cloud charges—a method that Hoff has dubbed an "economic denial of sustainability" (EDOS) attack.

Since cloud providers routinely host many virtual computers on the same physical system, experts think that in the next three years we'll also see cross-machine attacks, where a user creates a channel and injects data-stealing code into a neighboring VM on the same physical system. Or even worse, a VM user could inadvertently (or intentionally) download malware that targets the code for the cloud provider's manager program, which maintains the boundaries between VMs. The attack could wind up infecting all the other VMs under the manager program's control, or installing a backdoor that puts the entire system under the control of hackers.

Security researchers are working to come up with their own methods to defend against new malware attacks on the cloud. The innovations in the pipeline now will be vital for keeping all that data out of the wrong hands in the future. "As we move more services out to the cloud, we give criminals the ability to see 100,000 machines where there used to be just one. They find one small vulnerability, and it's game over," Joffe says. "It's an arms race, and right now the bad guys are winning."

5

Cloud Computing Could Minimize Security Threats

Armed Forces Communications and Electronics Association Cyber Committee

The Armed Forces Communications and Electronics Association (AFCEA) is a nonprofit organization that provides a forum for international exchange on issues relating to information technologies and security. The Cyber Committee is a select group of industry leaders and government liaisons that formulates strategies and responds to concerns regarding US national security.

Cloud computing may open up networks to a vast array of security threats. However, the same interconnectedness that allows for potential breaches also can also enhance security. Cloud servers and their operations are highly visible, meaning that they are easy to monitor, and security managers can amass data quickly from linked networks to respond to threats quickly. The linking of these cloud networks also means that various governmental and industry taskforces can share information and coordinate resources to address security issues collaboratively. Finally, the fact that cloud computing must constantly face security problems suggests that the next generation of information technologists will likely possess security training, creating a more educated workforce that is attuned to such threats and that can fashion a more secure cloud environment.

"Security and Cloud Computing," Armed Forces Communications and Electronics Association Cyber Committee, October 2011.

Security remains the number one obstacle to adoption of cloud computing for businesses and federal agencies. Public cloud solutions are seen as the most vulnerable options from a security perspective, leaving many federal customers to seek private alternatives to overcome security challenges. Regardless of the deployment model selected—private, public, community, or hybrid—conquering security concerns is required for cloud computing to achieve its full potential as the next generation of IT [information technology] architecture. Recent trends in cloud computing demonstrate the architecture has matured and offers distinct advantages for cyber security defense. Lessons learned continue to emerge with three areas of focus described here: visibility, collaboration, and workforce enrichment. . . .

Cloud Networks and Servers Are Highly Visible

Access to cloud computing services in traditional classified environments and in modern mobile environments provides numerous opportunities to gain visibility and retrieve security data points across your infrastructure, platforms, and applications. Collecting pulse points from the high-speed networks used to connect to your cloud provides insight into threats attempting to breach the perimeter of your infrastructure. Remote access devices and global position/location can be detected through other data points, triggering the requirement for additional security access and authorization controls while also providing real-time knowledge of the security status of end-user devices. Constant monitoring of applications and platforms offers additional data collection points for discovering vulnerabilities in applications that can be used to infiltrate the infrastructure. Moreover, merging measures and metrics from co-located environments or other cloud locations in your global enterprise can add yet another layer of data to the collection.

Establishing robust administrative and network management consoles designed to collate these numerous measures and metrics result in a level of security insight not previously achieved prior to cloud computing. Data points from routers, switches, firewalls, load balancers, storage networks, applications, and end-user devices combined with satellite, terrestrial, and wireless access methods allow true end-to-end security knowledge to identify, isolate, and eradicate breaches while minimizing impact and preserving mission.

New cyber security and IT service management products are emerging to provide real-time, deep insight of metrics collected in the cloud computing infrastructure. Visibility provided through new exploitation and analysis products will significantly enhance prevention of and rapid response to cyber intrusions.

Quick identification of potential breaches by either government or industry allows faster communication and broader dissemination of detailed information on exploitation, attack, or exfiltration attempts.

Utilities to migrate applications into the cloud provide other forms of visibility for security and application baseline management. Best practices for migration recommend a complete application inventory and analysis. The visibility derived from this inventory can be used to streamline legacy applications, accelerate implementation of common services, and confirm your organization's compliance with various continuity, disaster recovery, or legal reporting requirements. Structured virtualization migration processes contain code baseline inspections which can be used to identify assurance vulnerabilities in legacy applications. Overall, using a disciplined approach when implementing cloud computing optimizes your application baseline and improves your overall security posture.

Additional benefits derived from the cloud's ability to support robust collection of metrics is the parsing and analyzing of such data for other purposes. For example, individual usage patterns can be analyzed to a finer level of detail to support a variety of business purposes including enhanced customer experience and counterintelligence audit. Access to more granular performance data from all of the devices connected to your cloud allows deep analytics for load balancing refinement to support decisions on where and how to cache [store] data for best end-user support. You can drive more efficient usage of cloud resources with better understanding of available capacity based on real-time performance data. Finally, as a customer of cloud, the robust collection of metrics can provide dashboard views of your specific resource consumption thus allowing you to pay for only what you use with confidence.

Cloud Computing Facilitates Security Collaboration

Knowledge gained through improved visibility can be rapidly shared between government and industry to further widen the blanket of security protection. Quick identification of potential breaches by either government or industry allows faster communication and broader dissemination of detailed information on exploitation, attack, or exfiltration attempts. Widespread information sharing will appreciably improve the speed and depth of defensive response to enable broad spectrum protection of classified and unclassified information. Current computing architectures can limit visibility and sharing between government and industry—resulting in delayed reactions to breaches.

In the unfortunate event a serious cyber security incident occurs for government or industry, the vast collection of data from the cloud can be used for government-industry investigation. Inspecting massive amounts of information—stored and readily available—can accelerate understanding of an event, its consequences, and proper response. Government-industry partnerships also encourage comparison and validation of operating assumptions related to cyber security breach attempts and intrusions, thus enhancing progress on advanced defensive implementations.

Merging the IS and IT disciplines, combined with the development and implementation of formal and informal training programs to quickly increase the IS skill set of IT professionals, is absolutely necessary for the future.

The advantages of public-private partnerships extend beyond the improved visibility provided. Collaboration between government and industry means greater influence on regulatory and compliance requirements—the overwhelming majority of which were established in a non-cloud computing world. Working together, public and private organizations can drive policies in directions that promote future mission/business needs while also safeguarding our infrastructures and information. In addition, the partnerships can identify technical limitations in current cloud computing capabilities—whether security, performance, or utility—and drive improvements in products and architectures to overcome limitations. As an example, new non-hypervisor[1] based clouds are emerging in response to partnership pressures for better performance with "big data", computationally-intensive, and high-volume data collections that have not responded well to performance impacts created in the hypervisor layer.

Creating a New Workforce Attuned to Security Issues

Training tomorrow's IT workforce to rapidly identify and respond to cyber events requires new forms of traditional infor-

---

1. A hypervisor is a virtual platform that coordinates "guest" computers (running multiple operating systems) as they attempt to access a host computer.

mation security (IS) classroom training and innovative forms of on-the-job training. Cloud computing has highlighted weaknesses in traditional security training for our IT workforce. The plethora of data available through the many sensors described above can produce an overwhelming landscape of information that must be quickly analyzed and isolated to produce real-time defensive responses for IT teams. Merging the IS and IT disciplines, combined with the development and implementation of formal and informal training programs to quickly increase the IS skill set of IT professionals, is absolutely necessary for the future.

Academic programs should be shaped to create this blended workforce. Organizations will need to bridge the gap while universities produce the workforce with needed competencies. The bridge can be built initially by training the IT workforce on how to collate, assess, analyze, and respond to the insights generated through the cloud's many points of visibility. Use case scenarios based on real or fabricated intrusions can serve as excellent teaching tools and offer the added benefit of linking IT experts with junior IT professionals in a mentor program that can produce additional returns on the training investment.

IT administrators spend too much of their time performing security patch and maintenance operations, which detracts from time available for higher value contributions to the IT enterprise and for learning new tools/techniques. Cloud computing offers improved security by reducing requirements for global deployment of "fat" or "thick" client devices[2], which can be dangerous infiltration points and require constant patch management. Hard drives aren't necessary for access to cloud computing services, when such services are architected and implemented properly. End users can gain access to all in-

2. A fat or thick client device is a networked computer that performs operations independent of a server.

formation, applications, and services through thin client PCs, virtual desktop implementations, and wireless devices. This has an added benefit of improving corporate information security through rapid, near real-time deployment of security patches/upgrades. Moreover, the rapid deployment of patches gives administrators more time to learn new methodologies, perform deeper analysis of security events, and implement new processes to prevent future intrusions.

Creating Partnerships for Protection

Security obstacles surrounding cloud computing are being proactively addressed in a number of ways. Industry is creating partnerships to drive cloud computing standards and increase interoperability. Cloud computing alliances are forming to introduce innovative technologies designed to capitalize on the insights provided through cloud computing and produce enhanced cyber security awareness at all layers of the IT stack. Combining interoperability standards with improved cyber tools will give the IT workforce the capabilities needed to safeguard information and add value to mission.

6

A Cloud over Ownership

Simson L. Garfinkel

Simson L. Garfinkel is an author and researcher in Arlington, Virginia, who writes on technology issues relating to privacy and computer forensics.

Cloud technologies change the ownership of media content from consumer possession of physical objects to user access to personalized digital preferences. However, while users may purchase media content, they never own it exclusively. The content provider has ultimate control and may restrict or deny access as it sees fit. Currently, users have little recourse to legally challenge the "ownership" of cloud-based data. This must change. Users should have more clearly defined rights in this relationship, allowing them to move data, copy data, and secure data. Content providers also should be legally bound to respect the user's right to privacy over the content he or she examines or purchases.

Our possessions define us. Yet today the definition of possession itself is shifting, thanks to cloud services that store some things we hold dear on distant Internet servers. When those belongings reside in Netflix's video service, Amazon's Kindle bookstore, or Apple's coming iCloud service, they become impossible to misplace, and easier to organize and access than before. They also gain new powers over us, and slip free of powers we once held over them—powers that have shaped our thinking and behavior for centuries. One consequence is to give the companies that provide cloud services tremendous amounts of unchecked control over these possessions. In some cases, that control has already been abused.

Despite the supposed revolution wrought by digitization, mass computing has until now left the fundamental nature of our possessions untouched. Collections of content have adorned the shelves and walls of our homes, schools, and courts since the Enlightenment. Nearly all of us (who are old enough) collected vinyl records in the 1970s, videotapes in the '80s, CDs in the '90s, and DVDs in the '00s. Digitization simply morphed our urge to collect atoms into a thirst for curating bits, piled up on home computers.

The tattletale nature of things in the cloud comes from the fact that unlike practically every other object on the planet, cloud-things remain unbreakably tethered to their producer.

In this age of streaming, however, possessing a personal content collection is a logical inconsistency. The 200 movies in my Netflix instant queue form an aspirational list, not a personal collection. Once I actually watch a movie, it disappears from the queue—the reverse of what happens on my shelf of DVDs. Personalizing a cloud-based collection of content is a pale imitation of what physical possession can offer. Even were I to show dinner guests my Amazon Kindle account, they wouldn't gain the insight provided by a glance at a shelf in my dining room or the stack of books on my nightstand. There will never be a well-worn copy of my favorite digital book.

Dissolving physical possessions into the cloud is certainly convenient. It may even make us less covetous and more inclined to share. But this new form of property is also shaping up to have more serious consequences than the loss of a few conversations. One is that those previously inanimate possessions can now talk about you behind your back. Watch a movie on Netflix or Amazon, and the company's servers know who you are and what you watch, when you watch it, where you're watching from (more or less), and even when you fast-forward. U.S. law prohibits the release of movie titles that a person has watched, but cloud providers can do pretty much whatever they want with the other data they collect.

Today providers use this information to improve their service and make recommendations; tomorrow your data could travel to third parties. Apple could combine its own data with commercial data banks to tell Beyoncé the number of men aged 25 to 30 who are buying her tunes in New York City, for example; the music you place in Google's cloud storage and playback service could shape the advertising that you see all over the Web.

The tattletale nature of things in the cloud comes from the fact that unlike practically every other object on the planet, cloud-things remain unbreakably tethered to their producer. This tether means they bear little similarity to property as we have conceived it for hundreds of years. Popular understanding of what it means to own something—be it digital file or physical object—has up to now been well aligned with the law's. When you buy a book you don't get rights to the text, but you can read it, lend it to a friend, and then sell it to a secondhand shop, which can advertise it and sell it once more. But this tacit understanding of ownership is useless in the cloud.

Consider what happened in July 2009, when Amazon discovered it had accidently sold improperly licensed e-books of George Orwell's *1984* and electronically obliterated them from every Kindle in existence. [The book's protagonist] Winston Smith would have felt right at home, but the laws of physics, physical property, and copyright would have made such a maneuver triply impossible with a conventional book. Amazon could never have sent guards to conduct house-to-house searches.

In the cloud we are ruled by contract law and whatever constraints our provider builds into the long legal screeds we must agree to in order to use their services. Some aspects of these contracts are necessary for a company to operate. But they also provide an opportunity to place complex conditions on our possessions. Yes, you may lend Amazon e-books, but only for 14 days at a time. You may delete your e-books, but you can't give them to a friend when you are done reading them. Publisher HarperCollins has decided that libraries may lend out e-books only 26 times before they must purchase a new copy. Other publishers prohibit lending entirely. Amazon's Orwellian vanishing trick demonstrates that cloud providers have considerable power to enforce such rules. The nuclear option is the simplest restriction of all: terminating your account.

A fight with a cloud provider that controls so many of your digital possessions is a daunting prospect.

Back when you owned your own collection, you didn't risk losing it because you had a billing dispute with the Book-of-the-Month Club, nor could a library fine threaten your family photos. Such scenarios are becoming possible as cloud services become more consolidated. Apple's iCloud will look after e-mail, books, music, photos you take, and documents you create; Google's cloud services span the same range and now also include a Facebook-like social network, Google+. A fight with a cloud provider that controls so many of your digital possessions is a daunting prospect.

Threats to User Content

Threats to a carefree cloud come from outside, too. A hacker might steal or delete all your files, perhaps with the help of a screw-up like one that for a short time allowed users to log in to Dropbox cloud storage accounts with incorrect passwords.

When the bits and atoms that make up your possessions are safely inside your house, the security measures that matter are the locks on your doors and windows, and your own competence. When that property is online, a laptop anywhere in the world can steal your stuff.

Despite such dangers, the cloud cannot and should not be stopped. We have much to gain from the freedom it offers. We want to be able to access "our" content or creations from anywhere—even if the possessions we access that way are not really ours after all. We want the peace of mind that comes from knowing that if our house burns down or is robbed, many of the real things that matter won't be lost.

Yet not all the limits physical reality places on possessions are unfortunate. Many are pro-consumer and pro-freedom. Alas, those have been conveniently left behind by the largely unregulated market in which cloud providers operate. If we want the best of both cloud and physical possessions, we must find some way to rebalance the scales and reassert our rights.

Bolstering User Rights

Laws that force cloud providers to be humane landlords to those renting space on their servers, much as most U.S. states regulate landlords of physical space, would be a good place to start. Physical landlords can't have a tenant's possessions trucked off to the dump without due process; even those who withhold rent are given a chance to fight eviction in court. Cloud providers should similarly be prohibited from deleting your data at will, and there should be a legally mandated process for moving digital possessions to another cloud—or copying it to your home computer. Likewise, we need laws that force cloud providers to respect the privacy of their customers.

The industry currently has no incentive to allow us to negotiate our terms of service. When the laws of physics can no longer protect consumers and citizens as they have in the age of physical property, it is the obligation of society to intervene with the laws of man.

7

Cloud Technology Will Create Jobs

Sara Jerome

Sara Jerome is a technology correspondent for National Journal. *She previously worked as a technology policy reporter at* The Hill, *writing the "Hillicon Valley" blog.*

The shifting of content from personal computer hard drives to distant servers may suggest to some observers that industries with large information technology divisions may lose workers who are no longer needed to oversee those data. However, recent employment reports from businesses that utilize cloud storage indicate that the reverse is true. Cloud technologies are creating jobs worldwide as more companies, governments, and other institutions are following and developing the trend.

Here is an information-technology plan for the era of austerity: cloud computing. This innovation—namely, systems that store data on remote servers operated by host companies rather than on hardware owned by your employer—does away with expensive equipment and the hassle of maintaining it. So it's no surprise that the [Barack] Obama White House declared a "cloud-first" policy two years ago. The Office of Management and Budget said that if each department and agency moved just three projects to the cloud, the government would save $5 billion.

The trade-off, however, seemed to be that, in emancipating themselves from hardware, employers emancipate themselves from staff to support it. "[Our client was] able to eliminate a whole bunch of actually U.S.-based jobs and kind of replace them with two folks out of India to serve a 1,200-person engineering organization," gloated Richard Marcello, an executive at the IT [information technology] firm Unisys, at the Cloud Computing Conference & Expo in Santa Clara, Calif. A simple story of cutting spending at the expense of jobs, right?

Less Hardware but More Workers

Not so fast. If the story of cloud computing in the United States plays out as its backers promise, it could become one of the most successful recent job-creation trends. Cloud evangelists promise that a profitable new domestic industry will emerge from the ashes of the traditional IT model. "This is going to be a second version of the rise of the Internet. It's about to explode," says David LeDuc, senior director for public policy at the Software & Information Industry Association.

Economists haven't yet studied how this will all play out in the United States, but ... a British think tank ... predicts that the cloud market will create 2.4 million jobs over the next four years in Europe, the Middle East, and Asia.

It's true that, in this revolution, some tech professionals—particularly those focused on buying and running hardware—will lose their jobs. But the cloud isn't decimating IT departments. Recruiting firm Robert Half Technology found that, in 2009, 43 percent of chief information officers said that their departments are either "very" or "somewhat" understaffed. Unemployment for IT professions was just 5 percent in September, far less than the national average, and in a Microsoft study, 54 percent of IT decision makers said they are "hiring as a result of the cloud." At any rate, according to a report last year [2010] by the consultancy McKinsey, savings from cloud computing don't come from labor. An average business spends some $107 on labor each month for traditional storage, compared with $207 for Amazon's cloud, the report said. Lower costs come from less hardware, not fewer people.

Meanwhile, new jobs are sprouting up to service the cloud industry—and not just in the developing world. This new market, valued at $40.7 billion worldwide last year, is expected to reach $241 billion by 2020, according to a report this year [2011] by Forrester Research. Sure, some tech companies will base their servers overseas in low-cost environments, but the top cloud companies are American; all told, U.S. firms control 60 percent of the market, according to the latest data from 2009. "The massive computing infrastructure in the United States gives us an edge," LeDuc says. His trade association predicts that other countries will increasingly outsource their data to the United States, where Google and Microsoft keep many of their cloud servers.

Creating Jobs Worldwide

The cloud is already putting Americans to work. Google's team has more than 1,000 employees, Texas cloud company RackSpace employs 3,700 people, and California-based provider Saleforces.com has 235 open positions, according to *The Wall Street Journal*. U.S. businesses paid almost $22 billion to move to the cloud last year, and that figure is expected to rise to $80 billion by 2015, according to a study by IT consulting firm IDC.

Economists haven't yet studied how this will all play out in the United States, but the Center for Economics and Business Research, a British think tank, predicts that the cloud market will create 2.4 million jobs over the next four years in Europe, the Middle East, and Asia, with 300,000 alone in the United Kingdom. "Public and private organizations that preserve the status quo of wasteful spending [on IT] will be punished, while those that embrace the cloud will be rewarded with substantial savings and 21st-century jobs," Vivek Kundra, the former U.S. chief information officer who pushed the government into the cloud, wrote in *The New York Times* in August [2011].

The biggest hitch could be protectionism. Cloud providers such as Microsoft and Google are already working hard to prevent foreign governments from enacting laws banning "cross-border data flows." Such laws could force cloud companies to keep servers in the country where information originates rather than in the storage provider's country of choice. Kundra supports a global cloud policy "that forces nations to work together and resolve" cross-border issues. "The United States, along with leading nations in Europe and Asia, has an opportunity to announce such an initiative at the World Economic Forum meeting in January," he wrote in *The Times*.

Many consumers are already familiar with cloud technology (Gmail stores users' information on Google's huge servers rather than eating up the finite space on their laptops), and the federal government's buy-in has signaled that the cloud— once considered too vulnerable to cyberthreats—is now sufficiently secure for most offices. Washington spends $80 billion on IT each year, and tech officials hope to eventually move a quarter of that sum to the cloud. The payoff may take years, meaning that President Obama's policy won't affect today's unemployment rate. But if the cloud sector catches fire as promised, it will add, not subtract, American jobs.

8

Cloud Computing Will Destroy Jobs

Larry Dignan

Larry Dignan is editor in chief of ZDNet and SmartPlanet, two technology websites that are part of CBS Interactive. Dignan also serves as editorial director of ZDNet's sister site, TechRepublic.

The trend toward cloud computing is threatening jobs worldwide. As more companies adopt cloud storage and virtual interfaces, the need for a human workforce is diminishing. To increase profits, businesses that can take advantage of cloud computing will likely slash personnel to save on the costs of salaries and benefits. The end result may be a collapse of the oversaturated information technology job field.

Cloud computing, which amounts to be the industrialization of enterprise technology infrastructure, will bring a lot of advantages coupled with a lot of lost jobs.

Few disagree that cloud computing will be disruptive to industries, enterprise technology and the way we conduct businesses. The disruption will extend to the workforce.

In other words, humans will be virtualized just like servers are. The upshot from cloud computing is that companies will need fewer data centers. People run data centers. Those jobs are likely to simply disappear.

A Dire Prediction

Johan Jacobs and Ken Brant, two Gartner [a technology research firm] analysts, made the cloud computing-jobs connection last week at the Gartner Symposium in Orlando [Florida]. The presentation was categorized as "maverick" in that it may not happen in the allotted time frame. Jacobs and Brant argued by 2020 demand for IT [information technology] staff dedicated to supporting data centers will collapse.

"The long-run value proposition of IT is not to support the human workforce—it is to replace it," wrote Gartner in its presentation. In other words, any job loss related to offshore outsourcing may look like a walk in the park once cloud computing gets rolling.

The rough argument goes like this:

Computing will be outsourced to the cloud and become an IT utility. Business processes will be outsourced to software. That outcome will hit all economies—especially emerging ones like India that now dominate technology outsourcing. As the data center is virtualized the need for people to maintain that infrastructure will go away. In addition, all the people in sales and services linked to building and designing data centers will also lose jobs. When there's less technology infrastructure to support jobs will disappear. Some of those workers will reinvent themselves and find more opportunities. Others will never match those previous positions. Many IT workers will face hollowed out job prospects just like factory workers did as the U.S. manufacturing base disappeared.

This cloud computing-job connection is just a whisper today. But a few executives I talked to see an offshore outsourcing backlash as a possibility for cloud computing.

By worshipping profit ratios, companies nuke jobs.

If Gartner's post-human industry theory, which dictates that intelligent machines will drive the economy more than people, pans out the economic implications will be huge. There is no need for a human-machine singularity to impact career prospects. Creative destruction looks great on the whiteboard, but there is a human cost.

Heading Toward Full Automation

What's the probability for this cloud vs. jobs scenario? In the long run, I'd argue it's highly likely. The timing—2020—is debatable. Jacobs and Brant highlighted a few scenarios.

> If companies move to private clouds and hybrid infrastructure the job losses won't be as large. Companies will need to maintain people and use brokers for public cloud services. Machines may complement humans more than replace them. However, companies may aim to eliminate assets. Call centers will be run by avatars and software. Business operations will be largely automated. IT utilities emerge. IT utilities will accelerate asset cuts. In this scenario, the goal is to drop physical assets in a hurry.

The last two outcomes will have the most impact on jobs. This scenario ties into what Harvard professor Clay Christensen said last week [in October 2011]. Christensen noted that semiconductor companies tout how they are fables [i.e., they design and market semiconductors but outsource manufacturing]. As a result, Intel is one of the few that actually owns manufacturing facilities. By worshipping profit ratios, companies nuke jobs. In the long run, this focus on ratios hurts innovation.

Gartner noted that this ratio worship is already under way:

> CIOs [chief information officers] believe that their data centers, servers, desktop and business applications are grossly inefficient and must be rationalized over the next ten years. We believe that the people associated with these inefficient assets will also be rationalized in significant numbers along

the way. We foresee a substantial reduction in the U.S. IT workforce, especially among those supporting the data center and applications, in end-user organizations. According to Gartner's 2011 survey of U.S. CIOs, "Reducing the cost of IT," "Reorganizing IT" and "Consolidating IT operations and resources" were ranked high among their top strategies. In the same survey, "Virtualization" and "Cloud Computing" were the two top ranked U.S. CIO technology priorities; 83% of U.S. CIOs estimated that their organizations would conduct "more than half of their transactions on a cloud infrastructure" by 2020.

The other argument here is that IT is becoming a necessity good and that points to services provided by utilities. Toss in the fact that compensation is a large expense line in IT budgets and it's clear that there will be pressure to cut expenses via cloud computing and job cuts.

9

Cloud Computing Could Lessen Computing's Environmental Impact

Jack Newton

Jack Newton is the cofounder and president of Clio, a software-as-a-service company that provides web-based tools for legal firms.

Computer networks and servers are a mainstay of industry, and they account for a share of the world's power consumption. However, many of the servers in current use are not functioning at peak efficiency or, worse, they are sitting idle. If more businesses and institutions embraced cloud computing, which utilizes server space and coordinates processing more efficiently, then more work could be done with less power consumption. In addition, cloud computing can become even more environmentally friendly if it took greater advantage of low-emissions power sources, leading to an even greener future for information technologies.

Cloud computing and environmentalism are two of the most significant movements of the past decade. Although the two topics are often discussed separately, the ever-increasing impact of information technology (IT) on the environment can't be ignored. A recent McKinsey report estimates that IT, taken as a whole, produces nearly 1 gigaton of emissions a year, accounting for about 2 percent of total global emissions. The world's rapidly increasing demand for computation and data storage will see such emissions increase by the year 2020 to 1.54 gigatons, or 3 percent of global emissions, twice the total output of the United Kingdom today. By some estimates the emissions associated with IT will, by 2020, be greater than those associated with the airline industry. Although the ever-increasing demand for computing cannot be controlled, we must ask if there are ways we can deliver computing in a more efficient, environmentally friendly way. Cloud computing promises such efficiencies, giving rise to the natural question: Can moving more of our computational demands to the cloud help save the environment?

> *The inefficiencies of each business setting up an IT system that is, largely, identical to the IT systems of its peers echo the inefficiencies [automaker Henry] Ford saw in his predecessors' methods for assembling cars.*

Understanding the Cloud

Examining the underlying concepts and technologies that represent cloud computing will help clarify the broader effect cloud computing is likely to have on the environment.

The term "cloud computing" has been used broadly enough that its definition is accordingly nebulous, but it could be considered simply as a metaphor for the Internet (which is often, appropriately enough, depicted as a cloud in network diagrams). More specifically, cloud computing can be regarded as both an infrastructure and business model, where software and data, rather than being stored locally on your own servers and computers, are delivered to you in real time via the Internet.

Microsoft and Google, two pillars of the computing business, serve as a useful study in the transformational effect cloud computing is having on the industry. Microsoft has, traditionally, been an advocate of the "client-server" model of computing, where each business buys its own servers and workstations, purchases expensive software licenses for everything from file sharing to e-mail services to word processing, and hires IT staff to keep everything running. For the past 20 years this has been a wildly successful—and profitable—enterprise for Microsoft.

Conversely, Google, one of the pioneers of modern-day cloud computing, espouses a completely different model of computing. Rather than hosting e-mail and file servers on-premise, running database servers, and purchasing myriad software licenses, businesses simply use Google's products—such as Gmail and Google Docs—through a web browser. Google claims more than 2 million businesses have signed up for its cloud-based suite of products, and its adoption rate is only increasing. The swift consumption of Google's cloud-based services is now presenting a real threat to the Microsoft Office productivity suite, the company's most important revenue source after Windows. Microsoft's recently released Office 2010 is making an effort to combat Google by offering free cloud-based editions of Word, PowerPoint, and Excel.

Virtual Factories in a New Industrial Revolution

The underlying technological shift driving cloud computing in many ways parallels the forces at work during the industrial revolution. Prior to Henry Ford's pioneering work to centralize and streamline the assembly of vehicles, cars were assembled one-by-one by craftsmen in specialized shops. The advent of the modern assembly line ushered in an era of mass-produced, well-built, and affordable vehicles. The continued iteration and refinement of the assembly line process led Ford to build the world's first factories.

Similarly, the software and servers of the "client-server" computing model are set up one-by-one by the craftsman of a new generation: "the IT guy." The inefficiencies of each business setting up an IT system that is, largely, identical to the IT systems of its peers echo the inefficiencies Ford saw in his predecessors' methods for assembling cars.

Like the industrial revolution before it, the cloud computing-revolution centers around the concept of a factory. The factories are being built not by Ford, but by Google, Amazon, Apple, and Microsoft, and they produce one thing: computational power.

The innovation that underlies these cloud computing factories is a technology called "virtualization." Prior to the development of virtualization, each server tended to be dedicated to a given task. An e-mail server, for example, couldn't also act as a file server and as a database server. The reasons for this were often software- and performance-related, as the various server software products tended to interfere with each other and compete for system resources. As a result, system administrators tended to err on the side of conservatism and dedicate a server to a particular role, choosing performance and reliability over efficiency.

---

94 percent of the time servers are sitting idle—all while they continue to draw significant amounts of power.

Virtualization allows multiple "virtual machines" to be run on a single physical server. The individual virtual machines are completely isolated from one another, providing the performance and reliability benefits of a dedicated server while taking fuller advantage of the computation resources of the host physical server. If one virtual machine crashes, the other virtual machines will remain completely unaffected.

Virtualization is nothing new—IBM pioneered the concept in the 1960s—but its potential has only been fully realized with the development of massive new data centers. These new data centers, coupled with virtualization technology, allow for processing power to be purchased piecemeal, just as power can be purchased from the electricity grid. The transformation of computing into a utility that can respond with increased (or decreased) power to ever-changing, elastic demand is one of the defining traits of cloud computing.

Power Consumption for Idle Servers

For the typical on-premises IT system, there are more dirty secrets hiding in the server closet than you might guess. A McKinsey study found that, on average, server utilization is only 6 percent. This means that 94 percent of the time servers are sitting idle—all while they continue to draw significant amounts of power. The factors contributing to this underutilization include the "one task, one server" mentality that sees a powerful server dedicated to a single function. Additionally, servers are often more powerful than they need to be because they are purchased by businesses planning for tomorrow's needs. Lastly, and perhaps most obviously, most servers sit idle outside of the typical eight-hour workday.

A broad shift to cloud computing could, theoretically, result in a nearly 1.7-fold reduction in the number of servers required to meet 2011's computation demands.

Worse yet, the same study found that nearly 30 percent of servers worldwide are not used at all—skeletons of a disused IT infrastructure. System administrators, afraid of accidentally shutting down an important business function, simply leave servers running to be on the safe side.

The traditional client-server computing model and ever-decreasing costs of servers has resulted in the proliferation of servers in businesses of all sizes. Market research firm IDC predicts nearly 40 million servers will be in operation by 2011, up from 19 million in 2001.

Cloud Servers Run at Maximum Efficiency

The gross inefficiency of the traditional client-server model suggests the computational needs of these 40 million servers could be met with a mere 2.4 million servers operating at 100 percent capacity. Cloud computing, thanks to virtualization, operates servers at levels closer to their theoretical maximum. More importantly, however, cloud computing providers automatically power down servers and resources that aren't needed to meet current demand levels. A broad shift to cloud computing could, theoretically, result in a nearly 1.7-fold reduction in the number of servers required to meet 2011's computation demands.

Although cloud computing continues to be embraced by businesses large and small, universal adoption of cloud computing is unlikely ever to occur. Some businesses, owing either to regulatory requirements or internal policies, are unable or unwilling to leverage the public cloud computing resources offered by Amazon, Google, and others. However, these companies are taking advantage of virtualization to create their own data centers. These "private clouds" offer many of the same economic and environmental benefits of the public cloud while allowing companies to retain absolute control over their IT environment. HP is one company to have made the shift to private cloud computing; the company consolidated what used to be 85 data centers staffed by 19,000 IT workers to six cloud data centers with half the IT staff.

Power Sources for Server Centers

Cloud computing promises to dramatically reduce IT emissions by way of increasing server utilization and overall efficiency, but still more can be done to decrease the ecological impact of cloud computing infrastructure.

Although the term "cloud computing" evokes an almost ethereal image of an industry with little or no environmental impact, the physical infrastructure running the cloud has a very real, and growing, environmental footprint. The scale of cloud computing data centers is almost hard to imagine: Google is rumored to operate more than 1 million servers across three dozen data centers worldwide. Microsoft recently opened a new data center near Chicago that spans more than 500,000 square feet and holds 400,000 servers; the company is adding servers at a rate of 40,000 per month in an effort to catch up with Google. The Smart 2020 report by the Climate Group estimates energy consumption of these and other cloud data centers to be 330 billion kilowatt hours per year.

Cloud computing providers' desire for cheap energy must be aligned with environmentalists' desire for reduced emissions.

Because power is the primary cost associated with operating such data centers, companies choose to locate cloud data centers near cheap, plentiful, and reliable power. One of Google's largest data centers is located near Portland, Oregon, where inexpensive hydroelectric power is drawn from the Columbia River. As an added attraction, the area has much underutilized fiber optic capacity, a hangover of the dotcom era. Nearby Quincy, Washington, has attracted nearly a half-dozen data centers for the same reasons.

While hydroelectric power provides green energy to these particular data centers, most data centers derive their power from coal and other sources of dirty energy. Microsoft's massive data center near Chicago, for example, draws a mere 1.1 percent of its energy from renewable sources, according to a recent Greenpeace report. Similar data centers run by Google, Apple, and Yahoo! meet only 1 percent to 10 percent of their power needs with renewable resources.

Although cloud computing promised to dramatically reduce the number of servers required to meet the world's computing demands, the true challenge is to shift as much of the energy consumption of the cloud to green, zero-emission sources as possible. To accomplish this, the cloud computing providers' desire for cheap energy must be aligned with environmentalists' desire for reduced emissions. Taxes on emission-producing energy sources, whether by a cap-and-trade system or carbon tax, will accomplish this goal.

One of the primary drawbacks of green energy sources such as wind and solar farms is their requisite distance from major population centers. Transmission lines to major population centers are tremendously expensive to build, and up to 30 percent of the energy generated can be lost in transmission. But cloud data centers need not be near population centers. Locating cloud data center hubs near remote, zero-emission energy sources eliminates power line transmission losses and construction costs while providing cloud providers with several perks they factor into siting decisions: remoteness (for security reasons) and affordable land.

Reducing Environmental Impact

Cloud computing is the most energy-efficient method we have to address the ever-accelerating demand for computation and data storage. Although the architecture of cloud computing is an order of magnitude more efficient than traditional on-premises server solutions, the promise of truly green cloud computing lies with locating cloud data centers near clean, renewable sources of energy. Policy decisions that encourage the consumption of green energy sources will balance cloud computing providers' need for affordable energy with the need to reduce the overall environmental impact of cloud computing and will ensure that cloud computing is, in fact, green computing.

10

Cloud Computing Could Increase Computing's Environmental Impact

Simon Munro

Simon Munro is a senior practice consultant with EMC Consulting, a firm that helps businesses take advantage of cloud computing.

Cloud computing may be touted as a means to reduce the environmental impact of data processing and information transfer, but the system has its shortcomings. Because cloud computing is relatively inexpensive, industries that use its services may not feel the need to optimize efficiency or be concerned with the expense of running data during the hours of peak electricity demand. In addition, because cloud computing is so cheap, companies may run more programs—or less efficient ones—that make small net profits instead of optimizing performance and saving on the electrical costs. Cloud computing can be a green technology, but system architects and managers—and even government regulators—will have to find ways to compel businesses to be more efficient and responsible in running cloud-based applications.

Cloud computing is obviously green and good for the environment. For example,

- Computing power located near green resources—hydroelectric power or other renewable resources like they have in Iceland.

Simon Munro, "Environmentally Unfriendly Side Effects of Cloud Computing," *EMC Consulting Blogs* (blog), January 12, 2010. http://consultingblogs.emc.com. All rights reserved. Reproduced by permission of the author.

- Elasticity—resources don't have to sit around consuming power when underutilised and can be (virtually) spun up when required.

- Cloud computing makes use of commodity resources, reducing wastage and helping ensure that hardware components are used as long as possible.

So when vendors pitch cloud computing today, it seems a good idea to ride the one thing that may be hyped more than cloud computing—climate change, green energy and related topics. An environmentally responsible organization may want to do as much as they can to be more energy efficient (or at least make use of renewable energy resources) and cloud computing looks, on the surface, to be a good candidate.

In assessing the viability of cloud computing, running the numbers about how green it actually is for a particular usage scenario becomes a little bit more complicated than ticking off the green credentials. That is because cloud computing encourages behaviour that may not be very green. Like a Prius driver that commutes 2 miles a day instead of walking—just because the Prius is green technology, how it is used and applied is more important.

Environmental Pitfalls of Cloud Computing

I thought I would make up some potential non-green side effects of cloud computing . . .

- Availability of cheap resources encourages poor optimisation—It is easier and cheaper to throw another cheap server at a process than to code and debug a highly optimised solution.

- Processing during peak times—Because processors are available on demand, jobs that may have run at night can now be run any time, meaning that the energy required for processing is the most expensive and environmentally unfriendly.

- Over processing—Cloud computing allows things that may never have been processed before to be processed without an impact on performance, for example, selecting a very large set of data for analysis because you can literally process the data in an hour where previously it could have taken days.

- Providing low value products and services—If cloud computing lowers the cost to provide services, it is possible to provide services that only generate a few pennies per transaction. While generally considered a benefit of the cloud, one has to question whether the value of the end product is worth its environmental cost.

- Insisting on low latency—A big part of the greenness of cloud computing is the availability of resources where energy is cheaper (and more sustainable), but an over-zealous demand for low latency may mean that large data centres still need to be located in metropolitan areas where the environmental impact is high.

There is little doubt that some organizations can pull off very efficient (cloud) computing but I imagine that it is tough.

As we move from the 'why' in cloud computing to the 'how', claims about the green credentials of cloud computing need to to be clearly answered, motivated and calculated in order to substantiate the claims for a particular proposal. Reuven Cohen from Enomaly [a cloud computing service] has recently started asking these sorts of questions and makes a call for supporting data of the environmental friendliness of cloud computing—and seemingly finding very little.

Figuring Out the Best Strategies for Responsible Cloud Computing

There is little doubt that some organizations can pull off very efficient (cloud) computing but I imagine that it is tough. The efficient use of computing resources goes beyond the physical data centre and extends to the application architectures and usage scenarios around a potentially limitless and cheap supply of computing resources. My interest is to try and understand the influence of environmentally friendly approaches to application architectures and whether or not it is relevant. We could, for example, look at our application architecture and structure it to offload some processing (where latency [delay] is acceptable) to the most environmentally efficient data centre at that moment in time—say on the other side of the world where the data centre is making use of off-peak overcapacity. Of course, in the spirit of cloud computing, this should be done transparently and in a zero touch manner.

As Google found out a year ago with the furor that erupted over the estimated carbon footprint of a Google search, people are concerned about their energy consumption (or at least aware). Perhaps, with ever increasing public awareness of climate change, those same concerns will be directed at organizations, where responsible use of energy will become expected. It is possible that a few years down the line that regulators will jump in and require audits and aggressive increase in data centre efficiencies. With the current initiatives in building out new cloud computing oriented platforms, it would be prudent to spare a thought for the environment—if not in the implementation of energy efficient processing, then at least in the ability to measure whether or not we are successful.

Then can we use cloud computing as a platform to bring about the radical change in energy usage that is required to protect future generations from our insatiable appetite for computing resources.

11

New Legislation Must Address Specific Issues of Cloud Computing

Kurt Schiller

Kurt Schiller is a former assistant editor at Information Today, Inc., a company that provides resources and publishes periodicals concerning trends in information technology.

Because cloud computing companies perform operations and store data on servers in numerous locations across the globe, current legislation is inadequate to address the issues that may arise due to privacy concerns or even the recourse individuals and companies have in complaining about loss or misuse of data. Those using the cloud need to be guaranteed that their digital information is secure, and they should be able to demand that it is stored in specified locations. Only coordinated, international government regulation can succeed in setting up a framework to protect data and to offer a viable forum to redress violations.

In January 2010, Microsoft's senior vice president and general counsel Brad Smith made an unusual request. While speaking on a panel about cloud computing at the Brookings Institution, Smith stressed the growing importance of cloud computing to the audience of legislators and business-people. But what made Smith's address unusual is that he was not calling for fewer regulations in an emerging market; Smith and Microsoft were calling for more.

Microsoft is not alone in asking for legislation that clarifies the specifics of cloud computing. Despite the general tendency of corporations to battle against more restrictions, more companies and organizations are calling for new laws that govern this emerging technology. The reason is simple: Existing communications laws cannot adequately govern the modern internet.

Problems in the Cloud

Many of the laws that define the legal details of the internet and telecommunications are now decades old. Some, such as 1986's Electronic Communications Privacy Act, were drafted when most users still accessed the internet through company- or university-operated mainframes, and consumers didn't have access to the internet at all.

Today, things are very different, of course. Any user with a PC and an internet connection can gain access to the full run of the internet in no time. And with cloud services taking the place of more local software applications, even a task as simple as sending an email message might involve a half-dozen computers scattered in different locations around the country or even around the world.

The result is that existing computer laws drafted in the days of mainframes fall short when applied to modern issues of technology law. Questions of jurisdiction and privacy quickly arise: If a user sends an email from New Jersey to a user in Ohio using a cloud service based in New York, the question of the email's jurisdiction is better answered by a philosopher than a judge. If one of those users happens to be in another country, the result is a legal and jurisdictional quandary.

Blurring jurisdiction is quickly becoming a major problem with legal matters that involve cloud computing, according to Jorge Espinosa, an intellectual property lawyer with Espinosa Trueba, PL and author of cloud law blog LexNimbus. "In the

1990s, a lot of the services that were provided were still intra-territorial. They were within the United States from a U.S. perspective," he says. "So, yes, you still had privacy issues and security issues involving paying with credit cards and transferring e-mail. However, you knew that the data was located domestically, you knew that you had access to domestic law to seek remedies, and you didn't have to worry about order restrictions or export controls."

Although some cloud providers agree to confine computing services to a single country, this is far from the norm.

However, cloud computing changed all that. "One of the aspects of the cloud is that data can reside anywhere in the world," says Espinosa. "It can shift across international boundaries. And oftentimes in negotiating agreements, some of the larger providers like Microsoft refuse to restrict to single-country service providers."

Migrating Data and Security Concerns

For John Blossom, lead analyst and president of Shore Communications, Inc., cloud security is generating plenty of user attention. "In a world where your data could be anywhere in the world at any time, the need for these types of laws becomes more important," he says. "There will always be 'rogue states' that will not comply with international standards for security and legal prosecution of data theft, but the majority of nations that stand to profit most from cloud computing are now moving rapidly to establish laws such as those proposed in the Cloud Computing Act [broad legislation that calls for reform in the way the law handles cloud computing security and privacy]."

Although some cloud providers agree to confine computing services to a single country, this is far from the norm, and Espinosa notes that it may be out of the reach of smaller organizations to demand such terms. And because certain types of protected information, such as healthcare data, place strict controls on their disclosure and use, entire industries may be reluctant or unable to make use of cloud computing services.

"Until such laws are in place, it will be far more difficult for major information repositories housing private data to take full advantage of cloud computing's significant cost and service advantages," says Blossom. "Laws protecting the privacy of medical records such as HIPAA [Health Insurance Portability and Accountability Act], for example, will make many organizations hesitate to move toward cloud services until such standards are in place."

Privity and Middlemen

Espinosa says that another issue with cloud computing is a legal notion called privity, which "is a legal concept that says that I have a contractual relationship with you and that I have a right to take legal action against you for relief if you violate that contract," he says. "Well, oftentimes in a cloud context there are a couple of middlemen between you, the owner of the data, and the entity that is actually storing your data on a server somewhere."

> *The confusion over jurisdiction and policy specifics has made some companies wary of investing in cloud computing to a greater extent.*

If a legal situation arises due to the actions of a middleman, a business may not have the right to pursue legal action against the company or organization that is actually responsible for the loss or misuse of its data. If the organization responsible is outside the U.S., the question of local laws also comes into play, says Espinosa.

Espinosa notes that his own legal practice has been hindered in its attempt to use cloud technologies as a result of legal obligations. Because the firm could not get a guarantee from its cloud provider that storage would only take place within the U.S., it can only use the cloud solution in certain areas of the practice that don't involve sensitive information.

"That makes the cloud service less valuable to us, but at the same time we fulfill our obligations to our clients," says Espinosa.

Sharing Data and the Issue of Privacy

The confusion over jurisdiction and policy specifics has made some companies wary of investing in cloud computing to a greater extent, according to John Clippinger of the Massachusetts Institute of Technology's Media Lab. "There's a lot of expectation that things are going to be happening and moving to the cloud, but I think there's also a lot of reservation about what will be the governing legal regimes there, and what one can expect from different kinds of jurisdictions and what kind of policy of laws will prevail," he says. "There's just a lot of unknowns there, I guess, that people are uncomfortable in investing in it until they get resolved."

Clippinger's own work with cloud computing is over the issue of sharing and protecting personal information. "How do you develop and enforce different kinds of trust frameworks that provide compliant ways of meeting fair information practices in an interoperable environment? And that, to my mind, is one of the bigger issues that you're going to have in all cloud platforms," he says.

Clippinger notes that different jurisdictions, even within the U.S., have different sets of laws about sharing and protecting personal information. "The question is," he says, "when you're trying to run businesses across different jurisdictions, then what is going to be the prevailing set of principles? And in order to do that, I think you have to develop a different way of thinking about it that breaks with the traditional privacy/security model."

The National Strategy for Trusted Identities in Cyberspace (NSTIC) introduced one possible model—a proposal by the [Barack] Obama administration that aims to simplify certain aspects of internet privacy by creating a trusted system of on-line identity that could be used by businesses and the government alike. Shared standards for identity and privacy such as NSTIC could allow freer movement of data to the cloud while ensuring that protected data, such as healthcare information, is handled in a uniform and reliable fashion.

An International Matter

Blossom compares today's enterprise information resources in the cloud to "money in the bank." They can be "more securely managed in common repositories by security experts, more easily 'put to work' via data harvesting and aggregation services that can combine it with other information resources more readily, and more quickly translating their value into marketable advantages," he says. The global transparency required for corporate and state governance is also likely to push more information resources into the cloud, making it harder to cover up white-collar crimes. "Private enterprise computing services will focus increasingly on specialized 'big data' harvesting and analysis efforts," he says, "much as financial institutions do today for real-time securities markets analysis. . . ."

In April 2011, Sens. Amy Klobuchar, D-Minn., and Orrin Hatch, R-Utah, announced that they planned to introduce the Cloud Computing Act of 2011. Since the bill is still being drafted, specifics about its contents are difficult to ascertain. A draft of the bill was briefly leaked online but was quickly removed.

However, the senators have stated that the bill would address topics such as penalties for hacking cloud systems, and they encourage the U.S. to pursue international treaties covering cloud computing and data sharing. In many ways, the proposed bill seems to address many of the issues Microsoft's Smith initially pinpointed in his January 2010 presentation, although the final nature of the bill remains to be seen. (A Microsoft spokesperson declined to comment for this article.)

Although Espinosa says he cannot say for certain since he hasn't seen the text of the bill, he speculates that international treaties will likely be necessary to address the legal issues of cloud computing.

"A lot of our laws are out-of-date with how they handle everything from e-mail security to data transfers," says Espinosa. "However, when we're talking about the cloud, I think we need to appreciate that national solutions are never going to be fully adequate. What I mean by that is that the only way you're going to come up with a solution that adequately protects the growth and expansion of cloud computing is with a multinational approach."

But not all enterprises are rushing to the cloud. "In truth, it's not clear that even with such laws many major enterprises will ever put all of their 'crown jewels' of data resources out in cloud computing services," says Blossom. "However, as security and legal standards improve, it is becoming an increasingly compelling proposition."

Espinosa speculates that the future of cloud computing legislation may take the form of an international treaty such as the World Intellectual Property Organization (WIPO) Copyright Treaty, a 1996 treaty that standardized international intellectual property law and led to the U.S.'s Digital Millennium Copyright Act.

"You're going to have to have a group approach such as what we have with WIPO," says Espinosa. "Right now, if you want to challenge a URL used by somebody else, WIPO provides a streamlined process that whether you're in Germany, the United Kingdom, or the United States you can do. And it's simple, it works, and it's efficient. But it only works because Germany, the United Kingdom, and the U.S. are all signed onto this approach. If each country had its own rules for how you challenge a URL in that jurisdiction, you'd have a mess."

12

Too Much Legislation of Cloud Computing Could Stifle Innovation

Julian Sanchez

Former editor at the technology news site Ars Technica, Julian Sanchez is currently a fellow at the Cato Institute, a public policy organization devoted to free markets and personal liberty.

One of the enticing functions of cloud computing is the uploading and sharing of files with interested parties worldwide. Currently, some large companies are bringing suit against file sharing sites that may be in violation of copyright laws. While such claims may have validity, the US government already is heeding those complaints and shutting down sites before any legal trial has taken place. If the government can enact such powers, how can young file sharing companies that want to pursue cloud technology legally operate if they must spend so many resources on legal teams to police their users? And what guarantee do these startups have that the government will not arbitrarily close down their sites if some violation is perceived? This type of over-regulation in the service of large corporate interests will stifle innovation in cloud services and simply keep young companies from entering this valuable marketplace.

As I noted on Friday [January 20, 2012], the seizure of popular cyberlocker [third party file sharing sites] Megaupload demonstrates that, even without controversial new legislation, our government already has extraordinarily broad powers to take down U.S.-registered websites (including any site in the.com and.org domains) before anyone has been tried for illegal conduct, let alone convicted. While the evidence presented in the indictment charging Megaupload's executives with criminal racketeering and copyright infringement certainly seems damning, I also worried about the broader chilling effect such seizures could have on cloud storage services generally.

Criminalizing a Cloud Service

It didn't take long for those effects to become apparent. The cyberlocker Filesonic has now disabled file sharing functionality: Users can still upload files for personal storage, but can't create public links to enable others to access those files. (Though I'm not sure what prevents someone from simply creating a dummy account, uploading files, and then publicly posting the login information.) Another cyberlocker, Uploaded .to, is just blocking all traffic from U.S. Internet addresses, though it's not at all clear how much legal protection that's likely to afford them. You can hardly blame them for being skittish: The Megaupload indictment suggests that the U.S. government considers a wide array of cyberlocker business practices to be *ipso facto* evidence of criminal intentions, even though there are arguably legitimate reasons for many of them. Yet the government doesn't think it has to wait for a trial, or give the folks who run a site an opportunity to explain their practices, before seizing an entire domain—which would be an effective death sentence for many startups.

If you think all cyberlockers are nothing more than piracy tools, and there's no legitimate reason to make use of cloud storage for anything but personal backups, this might sound like an entirely healthy development. It's a little more worrying to those of us who see many valid reasons that law abiding individuals—even those who lack contracts with major record labels and movie studios, or the funds and tech savvy to run their own servers—might want to share large files with friends and colleagues, or distribute them to the general public.

Nobody's going to shut down YouTube or Twitter now, because we've already seen the incredible value creation they enable, even if they also make it a bit easier to infringe copyrights.

To be sure, such services aren't going to vanish entirely. Established corporations like Google have sophisticated filter algorithms that can help identify copyrighted content—though those are trivially defeated by file compression and encryption—and large, well paid legal teams to handle copyright compliance and fend off lawsuits, like the one Google's own YouTube continues to fight with content behemoth Viacom. The question is whether these are the *only* companies we want offering such services. Is the market for cloud-based platforms that enable sharing (which is *one of the big selling points of cloud computing*) a market we're prepared to see effectively closed off to startups that can't preemptively police every user-uploaded file to Hollywood's satisfaction? Because that is the predictable effect of a regulatory environment where investors know a nascent site can be summarily yanked offline by a district judge who thinks a Tumblr is some sort of gymnastics aficionado.

Stifling Innovation

If you're only thinking about current, known uses of the Internet, this might not seem like that big a deal: Why do we need lots of different platforms for sharing large files? But then, just a few years ago it was hard to envision why we might want a platform for sharing streams of 140-character messages ("Just a bunch of people gabbing about what they had for lunch, ho-ho-ho!") or a platform where anyone, not just Professional Content Creators, could upload short videos ("Amateur videos? Sounds like an excuse to steal movies!") or half the other technologies that are so profoundly shaping 21st century life.

The *last* innovation is always safe. That's why it's easy to claim concrete examples of the harm regulation might do are hyperbolic fearmongering: Nobody's going to shut down YouTube or Twitter *now*, because we've already seen the incredible value creation they enable, even if they also make it a bit easier to infringe copyrights. And anyway, the success stories eventually get big enough to afford their own fancy lawyers. It's the *next* platform that we risk strangling in the cradle, because every new medium starts out recapitulating old media content before it becomes truly generative. Early radio is full of people reading newspapers and books out loud. Early TV and film looks like what you get when someone points a camera at a stage play.

File lockers still look like nothing but piracy tools to a lot of people, because *most* of us aren't yet generating and sharing gigabytes worth of content on a daily basis. But it doesn't take a whole lot of imagination to imagine a world where that's not at all the case, a world where cheap, ubiquitous, powerful computing and rising bandwidth and falling storage costs make collaborative creation of high definition sound, video, and—who knows—maybe entire 3D environments a nigh universal recreational activity. (Like TV has been for the last couple generations, only with fewer dead brain cells.)

An Overregulated World

That world can be run by Google and Sony and a few other behemoths capable of negotiating byzantine licensing deals (and filtering protocols), with incumbents ill-disposed to see the value in anything that isn't easily shoehorned into their existing business models. Or we can have a more dynamic, open world where someone with a cool idea for a platform can give it a try without spending more money on lawyers than servers first. The interesting, important question isn't—as regulatory advocates want to make it—whether Megaupload should go out of business. Odds are it will and should, *after* a proper trial. It isn't even whether sites like Rapidshare or Hotfile ought to follow suit. The interesting, important question is whether we're going to have a *legal climate* that's capable of giving rise to the second kind of cultural ecosystem, or one that's only hospitable to the first kind.

13

Federal Policy Fosters Government Adoption of Secure Cloud Computing

David McClure

David McClure is the associate administrator of the US General Services Administration Office of Citizen Services and Innovative Technologies. His department is charged with making government information technologies more accessible and transparent by taking advantage of new technologies that speed distribution and availability of public information.

As the government tries to cut expenses and streamline technology, various agencies should avail themselves of cloud computing services. However, to ensure that these third-party services are secure and necessary, the Government Services Administration is instituting the Federal Risk Authorization Management Program (FedRAMP) in 2012. FedRAMP is an interagency operation that will facilitate and coordinate adoption of cloud services. It will authorize and accredit service providers to ensure security of government data, and it will provide oversight of the providers and assess any risks that arise. Transitioning to cloud computing will reduce government expenditure on servers, storage, and personnel, and security will likely improve as a chief function of providers is to monitor threats and issue feedback continuously.

David McClure, "Cloud Computing: What Are the Security Implications," Testimony Before the Subcommittee on Cybersecurity, Infrastructure Protection, and Security Technologies, Committee on Homeland Security, House of Representatives, October 6, 2011.

Before I discuss the security of cloud computing, and the Federal Risk Authorization and Management Program (FedRAMP) in particular, I would like to make two important points. First, cloud computing offers a compelling opportunity to substantially improve the efficiency of the federal government. It moves us from buying and managing physical assets to purchasing IT [information technology] as a commoditized service. Agencies pay for only IT resources they use in response to fluctuating program demands, avoiding the expenses of building and maintaining costly IT (information technology) infrastructure. When implemented with sound security risk management approaches, cloud computing also ensures more consistent protection of the government's IT infrastructure, data and applications.

Second, practical use of cloud computing offers substantial performance benefits for the government. Federal agencies are moving to consolidate and virtualize the more than 2,000 federal data centers. Cloud technologies provide an ideal path forward to maximize value in IT investment dollars while substantially lowering costs—an essential focus given federal budget constraints. Case studies we have collected from agencies point to benefits that include:

- tangible cost reductions (data storage, web hosting and analytics performed on the government's vast data repositories);

- enhanced productivity (shifting workforce to more high value process improvements, problem solving, and customer service excellence);

- greater flexibility and scalability (enabling CIOs [chief information officers] to be much more responsive to pressing service delivery expectations); and

- improved self-service capabilities (on-line streamlined commodity-like purchasing for IT resources rather than long, arduous IT acquisitions).

The Feasibility of Adopting Cloud Services for Government Use

GSA [US General Services Administration] is playing a leadership role in facilitating easy access to cloud-based solutions from commercial providers that meet federal requirements. This will enable agencies to analyze viable cloud computing options that meet their business and technology modernization needs, while reducing barriers to safe and secure cloud computing. We are developing new cloud computing procurement options with proven solutions that leverage the government's buying power. These cloud procurement vehicles ensure effective cloud security and standards are in place to lower risk and foster government-wide use of cloud computing solutions such as virtualization technologies for government data centers, cloud email, disaster recovery/backup, and infrastructure storage. Useful information about cloud computing and available solutions is accessible from our web page. Info.Apps.gov.

GSA's Federal Cloud Computing Initiative was started and is managed under GSA's e-Government program. In FY10 and FY11 GSA's Federal Cloud Computing Initiative (FCCI) Program Management Office (PMO) focused on five primary tasks:

- Establishing procurement vehicles that allow agencies to purchase IT resources as commodities, culminating in the award of the Infrastructure as a Service (IaaS) Blanket Purchase Agreement under GSA Schedule 70 to 12 diverse cloud service providers

- Addressing security risks in deploying government information in a cloud environment—resulting in the development of the Federal Risk Authorization Management Program (FedRAMP)

- Establishing a procurement vehicle that will allow agencies to purchase cloud-based e-mail services, which created GSA's Email as a Service (EaaS) Blanket Purchase Agreement

- Supporting the government-wide collection and assessment of data center inventories, and assisting agencies in the preparation and execution of plans to close and consolidate data centers. Current work includes developing a comprehensive data center Total Cost Model for agencies to use to analyze alternative consolidation scenarios, enables data-driven decision-making for infrastructure cost and performance optimization. Operationalizing a data center marketplace that would help optimize infrastructure utilization across government by matching agencies with excess computing capacity with those that have immediate requirements is also being pursued

- Creating apps.gov, an on-line storefront that provides access to over 3,000 cloud-based products and services where agencies can research solutions, compare prices and place on-line orders using GSA's eBuy system Initial funding provided by the e-Gov Fund has allowed GSA to be an effective catalyst for secure cloud technology adoption governmentwide.

The primary goal of the Administration's Cloud First policy is to achieve widespread practical use of secure cloud computing to improve operational efficiency and effectiveness of government.

However, there are critical activities that still need to be accomplished to fully realize the significant cost savings and productivity improvements that GSA can help agencies achieve. The continuation of these cost-saving initiatives is dependent on FY12 eGov Fund budget levels and decisions.

FedRAMP: Ensuring Secure Cloud Systems Adoption

Cloud computing—like any technology—presents both known and new risks alongside the many benefits outlined above. To address these risks in a more uniform and comprehensive manner, we will soon launch a new government-wide cloud security program—the Federal Risk and Authorization Management Program (FedRAMP). The primary goal of the Administration's Cloud First policy is to achieve widespread practical use of secure cloud computing to improve operational efficiency and effectiveness of government. Today, each agency typically conducts its own security Certification and Accreditation (C&A) process for every IT system it acquires, leading to unnecessary expense, duplication and inconsistencies in the application of NIST [National Institute of Standards and Technology] derived security controls testing, evaluation, and certification procedures. According to the 2009 FISMA [Federal Information Security Management Act of 2002] report to Congress, agencies reported spending $300 million annually on C&A activities alone.

FedRAMP approves qualified, independent third party security assessment organizations, ensuring consistent assessment and accreditation of cloud solutions based on NIST's longstanding conformity assessment approach.

At GSA, we have worked in close collaboration with cybersecurity and cloud experts in NIST, DHS [Department of Homeland Security], DoD [Department of Defense], NSA [National Security Agency], OMB [Office of Management and Budget], and the Federal CIO Council and its Information Security and Identity Management Subcommittee (ISIMC) to develop FedRAMP. An OMB policy memo officially establishing the FedRAMP program is expected shortly. The intent is to strengthen existing security practices associated with cloud computing solutions which, in turn, will build greater trust between providers and consumers and accelerate appropriate adoption of secure cloud solutions across government. Accordingly, FedRAMP establishes a common set of baseline security assessment and continuous monitoring requirements for FISMA low and moderate impact risk levels using NIST standards that must be adhered to by all cloud systems. . . .

Ensuring Consistency and Quality in Cloud Security Certification and Accreditation

FedRAMP approves qualified, independent third party security assessment organizations, ensuring consistent assessment and accreditation of cloud solutions based on NIST's long-standing conformity assessment approach. As noted above, security C&As are currently performed with varying quality and consistency. This is true for situations where a third party service provider is contracted to do a security assessment of a CSP [cloud service provider] provided system, product or service and where government security organizations perform the work themselves. As a result, trust levels are low for reusing this work across agencies.

To address this challenge, FedRAMP will require that cloud service providers be assessed using these approved, independent third party assessment organizations (3PAOs). The 3PAOs will initially apply for accreditation through the FedRAMP PMO [project management office] and be assessed using established conformity assessment criteria developed by NIST. This will ensure higher quality assessments, done much more consistently, using agreed upon FedRAMP security assessment controls. This can save millions of dollars in expenses borne both by government and industry in running duplicative assessments of similar solutions by each agency.

Building Trust and Reusing Existing Certification and Accreditation Work

All IT systems, including cloud solutions, must receive an Authority to Operate (ATO) from the buying agency before they can be made available for purchase and implemented. The ATO is based on a thorough review by agency security professionals of the security packages submitted following the C&A process described above. To accelerate cloud adoption and enable C&A re-use, FedRAMP will provide a single, provisional authorization that can be used by all agencies as the basis for issuing an ATO. If additional security assessment evaluation and testing is needed for specific agency cloud implementations, the C&A should only address any additional controls needed above the existing FedRAMP approved baseline.

> *FedRAMP shifts risk management from annual reporting . . . to more robust continuous monitoring, providing real-time detection and mitigation of persistent vulnerabilities and security incidents.*

FedRAMP establishes a Joint Authorization Board (JAB) that reviews all cloud systems that have been assessed by approved 3PAOs using FedRAMP controls and processes. The JAB membership consists of CIOs and Technical Representatives from DOD, DHS, and GSA. The JAB reviews the C&A work and decides whether to grant the "provisional authorization"—a seal of approval on the C&A work. The security packages, assessments and documented decisions will be accessible within government from a secure central repository. While each agency must grant its own ATO for systems under its control, FedRAMP will facilitate greater use of an "approve once, and use often" approach, leveraging more ATOs across government.

Moving Toward More Real-Time Security Assurance

FedRAMP shifts risk management from annual reporting under FISMA to more robust continuous monitoring, providing real-time detection and mitigation of persistent vulnerabilities and security incidents. Using the expertise of industry, NIST, NSA, DHS and ISIMC, nine initial continuous monitoring controls have been identified that are among the most common persistent threat vulnerabilities in cloud and non-cloud systems environments. Cloud Service Providers (CSPs) must agree to near-real time reporting of continuous monitoring data feeds to DHS and/or agency Security Operations Centers (SOCs). We are finalizing data reporting details, with the expectation that the process will eventually use automated data feeds to maximize efficiencies and timeliness. When done in addition to the C&A evaluations, this will result in valuable situational cyber awareness—a relevant and timely picture of a CSP's security posture. In addition, this approach provides visibility of prompt mitigation and tangible evidence of resolution: ensuring quick steps are taken to minimize threats to government data and operations.

There is strong support and demand for stronger cloud security from agencies seeking to adopt cloud services, as required by the Administration's Cloud First policy. Industry cloud services providers need to know the specific cloud security capabilities for which they are accountable. They also desire more efficiency in how C&As and ATOs are leveraged government-wide to avoid unnecessary, duplicative, costly security evaluations. Ensuring IT security is an ongoing challenge. We fully expect to make improvements to the process based on collaboration with all key stakeholders, including industry, lessons learned and the continuous evolution of security standards and controls based upon the careful, deliberative work of NIST.

FedRAMP will be launched in phases that incrementally build toward sustainable operations and allow for risk management by capturing ongoing lessons learned and process improvement. Initial rollout will occur this Fall [2011]. Initial Operational Capabilities will have limited scope and cover a relatively small number of cloud service providers. Full operations are expected to begin next Spring with more robust operational capabilities and larger intake of cloud service providers for FedRAMP review and approval.

Late in 2012, we expect sustaining operations to scale by demand using a privatized board for 3PAO accreditation. We will discuss the rollout in more depth with the Congress, government executive branch agencies, industry, and the public prior to the initial launch date.

A Roadmap for Government Agencies

Considerable progress has been made in adopting successful cloud solutions. Cloud computing is now an accepted part of the federal IT lexicon. However, there continues to be a need for more thorough understanding of cloud deployment models, unique security implications, and data management challenges. Agency executives should not focus on cloud technology itself; rather, they should focus on the desired outcome driving the need for cloud adoption delivered in a secure environment.

FedRAMP will provide a sound, cost-effective framework for secure cloud computing. CIOs need to work with their line of business executives and program managers to develop and deploy effective cloud roadmaps that address pressing agency mission needs, taking into account appropriate security and risk management. Agencies should analyze business needs and identify cloud solutions that best fit their requirements by making secure cloud adoption part of an overall IT portfolio management and sourcing strategy. Consistent with the Federal Cloud Computing Strategy, NIST is currently working on the first draft of a USG Cloud Computing Technology Roadmap, to be released for public comment in November, 2011. If linked to cloud provider products and services, it would greatly assist in this decision-making.

14

Improvement Needed Before Government's Adoption of Cloud Computing

Gregory C. Wilshusen

Gregory C. Wilshusen joined the US Government Accountability Office in 1997. After working in a number of posts, he now serves as the director of Information Security Issues.

As various government agencies move toward the adoption of cloud computing, data security remains the chief priority. While several agencies have begun establishing protocols for dealing with nongovernmental vendors of cloud services, these efforts still face unaddressed challenges and lack any kind of interagency coordination. Policies exist as a patchwork and some government organizations have not moved beyond the planning stages in drafting security guidelines. Until clear guidelines are finalized, these agencies cannot successfully respond to the concerns and risks posed by cloud technology.

Cloud computing, an emerging form of delivering computing services, can, at a high level, be described as a form of computing where users have access to scalable, on-demand information technology (IT) capabilities that are provided through Internet-based technologies. Examples of cloud computing include Web-based e-mail applications and common business applications that are accessed online through a

Gregory C. Wilshusen, "Information Security: Additional Guidance Needed to Address Cloud Computing Concerns," Testimony Before the Subcommittee on Cybersecurity, Infrastructure Protection, and Security Technologies, Committee on Homeland Security, House of Representatives, October 6, 2011.

browser, instead of through a local computer. Cloud computing can potentially deliver several benefits over current systems, including faster deployment of computing resources, a decreased need to buy hardware or to build data centers, and more robust collaboration capabilities. However, along with these benefits are the potential risks that any new form of computing services can bring, including information security breaches, infrastructure failure, and loss of data. Media reports have described security breaches of cloud infrastructure and reports by others have identified security as the major concern hindering federal agencies from adopting cloud computing services. . . .

We [at the Government Accountability Office, or GAO] have previously reported that cyber threats to federal information systems and cyber-based critical infrastructures are evolving and growing. Without proper safeguards, computer systems are vulnerable to individuals and groups with malicious intentions who can intrude and use their access to obtain and manipulate sensitive information, commit fraud, disrupt operations, or launch attacks against other computer systems and networks.

In addition, the increasing interconnectivity among information systems, the Internet, and other infrastructure presents increasing opportunities for attacks. For example, since 2010, several media reports described incidents that affected cloud service providers such as Amazon, Google, and Microsoft. Additional media reports have described hackers exploiting cloud services for malicious purposes. The adoption of cloud computing will require federal agencies to implement new protocols and technologies and interconnect diverse networks and systems while mitigating and responding to threats.

Our previous reports and those by agency inspectors general describe serious and widespread information security control deficiencies that continue to place federal assets at risk of inadvertent or deliberate misuse, mission-critical information at risk of unauthorized modification or destruction, sensitive information at risk of inappropriate disclosure, and critical operations at risk of disruption. We have also reported that weaknesses in information security policies and practices at major federal agencies continue to place confidentiality, integrity, and availability of sensitive information and information systems at risk. Accordingly, we have designated information security as a governmentwide high-risk area since 1997, a designation that remains in force today. To assist agencies, GAO and agency inspectors general have made hundreds of recommendations to agencies for actions necessary to resolve control deficiencies and information security program shortfalls.

Cloud Computing's Service Models

Cloud computing delivers IT (information technology) services by taking advantage of several broad evolutionary trends in IT, including the use of virtualization.[1] According to NIST [National Institute of Standards and Technology], cloud computing is a means "for enabling convenient, on-demand network access to a shared pool of configurable computing resources that can be rapidly provisioned and released with minimal management effort or service provider interaction." NIST also states that an application should possess five essential characteristics to be considered cloud computing: on-demand self service, broad network access, resource pooling, rapid elasticity, and measured service.

Cloud computing offers three service models: infrastructure as a service, where a vendor offers various infrastructure components; platform as a service, where a vendor offers a ready-to-use platform on which customers can build applica-

---

1. Virtualization is a technology that allows multiple software-based virtual machines with different operating systems to run in isolation, side-by-side on the same physical machine. Virtual machines can be stored as files, making it possible to save a virtual machine and move it from one physical server to another.

tions; and software as a service, which provides a self-contained operating environment used to deliver a complete application such as Web-based e-mail. . . .

In response to our survey, 22 of 24 major agencies reported that they are either concerned or very concerned about the potential information security risks associated with cloud computing.

In addition, four deployment models for providing cloud services have been developed: private, community, public, and hybrid cloud. In a private cloud, the service is set up specifically for one organization, although there may be multiple customers within that organization and the cloud may exist on or off the premises. In a community cloud, the service is set up for related organizations that have similar requirements. A public cloud is available to any paying customer and is owned and operated by the service provider. A hybrid cloud is a composite of the deployment models. . . .

Agency Concerns About Cloud Computing

Cloud computing can both increase and decrease the security of information systems. Potential information security benefits include the use of virtualization and automation to expedite the implementation of secure configurations for virtual machine images. Other advantages relate to cloud computing's broad network access and use of Internet-based technologies. For example, several agencies stated that cloud computing provides a reduced need to carry data in removable media because of the ability to access the data through the Internet, regardless of location. In response to the survey we conducted for our 2010 report, 22 of the 24 major agencies also identified low-cost disaster recovery and data storage as a potential benefit.

The use of cloud computing can also create numerous information security risks for federal agencies. In response to our survey, 22 of 24 major agencies reported that they are either concerned or very concerned about the potential information security risks associated with cloud computing. Several of these risks relate to being dependent on a vendor's security assurances and practices. Specifically, several agencies stated concerns about

- the possibility that ineffective or noncompliant service provider security controls could lead to vulnerabilities affecting the confidentiality, integrity, and availability of agency information;

- the potential loss of governance and physical control over agency data and information when an agency cedes control to the provider for the performance of certain security controls and practices; and

- potentially inadequate background security investigations for service provider employees that could lead to an increased risk of wrongful activities by malicious insiders.

Of particular concern was dependency on a vendor. All 24 agencies specifically noted concern about the possibility of loss of data if a cloud computing provider stopped offering its services to the agency. For example, the provider and the customer may not have agreed on terms to transfer or duplicate the data.

Multitenancy, or the sharing of computing resources by different organizations, can also increase risk. Twenty-three of 24 major agencies identified multitenancy as a potential information security risk because, under this type of arrangement, one customer could intentionally or unintentionally gain access to another customer's data, causing a release of sensitive information. Agencies also stated concerns related to exchanging authentication information on users and responding to security incidents. Identity management and user authentication are a concern for some government officials because customers and a provider may need to establish a means to securely exchange and rely on authentication and authorization information for system users. In addition, responding to security incidents may be more difficult in a shared environment because there could be confusion over who performs the specific tasks—the customer or the provider.

Agencies identified measures they were taking or planned to take when using cloud computing. These actions, however, had not always been accompanied by development of related policies or procedures.

Although there are numerous potential information security risks related to cloud computing, these risks may vary based on the particular deployment model. For example, NIST stated that private clouds may have a lower threat exposure than community clouds, which may have a lower threat exposure than public clouds. Several industry representatives stated that an agency would need to examine the specific security controls of the provider the agency was evaluating when considering the use of cloud computing.

Security Plans Are Yet to Be Realized or Coordinated

In our report, we noted that federal agencies had begun to address information security for cloud computing; however, they had not developed corresponding guidance. About half of the 24 major agencies reported using some form of public or private cloud computing for obtaining infrastructure, platform, or software services. These agencies identified measures they were taking or planned to take when using cloud computing.

These actions, however, had not always been accompanied by development of related policies or procedures.

Most agencies had concerns about ensuring vendor compliance and implementation of government information security requirements. In addition, agencies expressed concerns about limitations on their ability to conduct independent audits and assessments of security controls of cloud computing service providers. Several industry representatives were in agreement that compliance and oversight issues were a concern and raised the idea of having a single government entity or other independent entity conduct security oversight and audits of cloud computing service providers on behalf of federal agencies. Agencies also stated that having a cloud service provider that had been precertified as being in compliance with government information security requirements through some type of governmentwide approval process would make it easier for them to consider adopting cloud computing. Other agency concerns related to the division of information security responsibilities between customer and provider. As a result, we reported that the adoption of cloud computing by federal agencies may be limited until these concerns were addressed.

Challenges and Delays in Meeting Objectives

In our May 2010 report, we also noted that several governmentwide cloud computing security activities had been undertaken by organizations such as the Office of Management and Budget (OMB), General Services Administration (GSA), the federal Chief Information Officers (CIO) Council, and NIST; however, significant work remained to be completed. Specifically, OMB had stated that it had begun a federal cloud computing initiative in February 2009; however, it did not have an overarching strategy or an implementation plan. In addition, OMB had not yet defined how information security issues, such as a shared assessment and authorization process, would be addressed.

GSA had established the Cloud Computing Program Management Office, which manages several cloud computing activities within GSA and provides administrative support for cloud computing efforts by the CIO Council. The program office manages a storefront, www.apps.gov, established by GSA to provide a central location where federal customers can purchase software as a service cloud computing applications. GSA had also initiated a procurement to expand the storefront by adding infrastructure as a service cloud computing offerings such as storage, virtual machines, and Web hosting. However, GSA officials reported challenges in addressing information security issues as part of the procurement. As a result, in early March 2010, GSA canceled the request and announced plans to begin a new request process. GSA officials stated that they needed to work with vendors after a new procurement was completed to develop a shared assessment and authorization process for customers of cloud services purchased as part of the procurement, but had not yet developed specific plans to do so.

Both federal and private sector officials had made clear that existing [NIST] guidance [on cloud computing security] was not sufficient.

In addition to GSA's efforts, the CIO Council had established a cloud computing Executive Steering Committee to promote the use of cloud computing in the federal government, with technical and administrative support provided by GSA's Cloud Computing Program Management Office, but had not finalized key processes or guidance. A subgroup of this committee had developed the Federal Risk and Authorization Management Program (FedRAMP), a governmentwide program to provide joint authorizations and continuous security monitoring services for all federal agencies, with an initial focus on cloud computing. The subgroup had worked with its members to define interagency security requirements for cloud systems and services and related information security controls. However, a deadline for completing development and implementation of a shared assessment and authorization process had not been established.

Until [specific] challenges are addressed, agencies may have difficulty readily adopting cloud computing technologies.

NIST is responsible for establishing information security guidance for federal agencies to support the Federal Information Security Management Act of 2002 (FISMA); however, at the time of our report, it had not yet established guidance specific to cloud computing or to information security issues specific to cloud computing, such as portability, interoperability, and visualization. The NIST official leading the institute's cloud computing activities stated that existing NIST guidance in Special Publication (SP) 800-53 and other publications applied to cloud computing and could be tailored to the information security issues specific to cloud computing. However, both federal and private sector officials had made clear that existing guidance was not sufficient.

Effort Is Needed to Complete Vital Tasks

In our May 2010 report, we made several recommendations to OMB, GSA, and NIST to assist federal agencies in identifying uses for cloud computing and information security measures to use in implementing cloud computing. These agencies generally agreed with our recommendations. Specifically, we recommended that the Director of OMB establish milestones for completing a strategy for implementing the federal cloud computing initiative; ensure the strategy addressed the information security challenges associated with cloud computing, such as needed agency-specific guidance, the appropriate use of attestation standards for control assessments of cloud computing service providers, division of information security responsibilities between customer and provider, the shared assessment and authorization process, and the possibility for precertification of cloud computing service providers; and direct the CIO Council Cloud Computing Executive Steering Committee to develop a plan, including milestones, for completing a governmentwide security assessment and authorization process for cloud services.

In response, in February 2011, OMB issued its *Federal Cloud Computing Strategy*, which references the establishment of a shared assessment and authorization process for cloud computing. In addition, the strategy discusses other steps to promote cloud computing in the federal government, including ensuring security when using cloud computing, streamlining procurement processes, establishing standards, recognizing the international dimensions of cloud computing, and establishing a governance structure. However, the strategy does not address other security challenges such as needed agency-specific guidance, the appropriate use of attestation standards for control assessments of cloud computing service providers, and the division of information security-related responsibilities between customer and provider. Until these challenges are addressed, agencies may have difficulty readily adopting cloud computing technologies.

We also recommended that the Administrator of GSA, as part of the procurement for infrastructure as a service cloud computing technologies, ensure that full consideration be given to the information security challenges of cloud computing, including a need for a shared assessment and authorization process.

In response, GSA issued a request for quote relating to its procurement for cloud services that included the need to use FedRAMP once it is operational. FedRAMP was further developed by GSA, in collaboration with the Cloud Computing Executive Committee, as a shared assessment and authorization process to provide security authorizations and continuous monitoring for systems shared among federal agencies. The CIO Council, in collaboration with GSA, issued a draft version of the shared assessment and authorization process in November 2010; however, the process has not yet been finalized. GSA officials stated that they intend to release additional information on FedRAMP once OMB issues a policy memorandum related to cloud computing, expected in the first quarter of fiscal year 2012.

Lastly, to assist federal agencies in implementing appropriate information security controls when using cloud computing, we recommended that the Secretary of Commerce direct the Administrator of NIST to issue cloud computing information security guidance to federal agencies to more fully address key cloud computing domain areas that are lacking in SP 800-53, such as virtualization, data center operations, and portability and interoperability, and include a process for defining roles and responsibilities of cloud computing service providers and customers.

NIST has also taken steps to address our recommendations. In January 2011, it issued SP 800-125, *Guide to Security for Full Virtualization Technologies*. Virtualization is a key technological component of cloud computing. SP 800-125 discusses the security characteristics of virtualization technologies, provides security recommendations for virtualization components, and highlights security considerations throughout the system life cycle of virtualization solutions. In July 2011, NIST issued SP 500-291, *NIST Cloud Computing Standards Roadmap*, and in September 2011, SP 500-292, *NIST Cloud Computing Reference Architecture*. Collectively these documents provide guidance to help agencies understand cloud computing standards and categories of cloud services that can be used governmentwide. Among other things, these publications address cloud computing standards for interoperability and portability.

NIST also issued a draft publication on cloud computing, SP 800-144, *Guidelines on Security and Privacy in Public Cloud Computing*, which addresses the security concerns associated with data center operations and the division of responsibilities among providers and customers. In addition, the guide discusses the benefits and drawbacks of public cloud computing, precautions that can be taken to mitigate risks, and provides guidance on addressing security and privacy issues when outsourcing support for data and applications to a cloud provider. According to NIST officials, SP 800-144 will be finalized in the first quarter of fiscal year 2012.

There Is Much to Be Done

In summary, the adoption of cloud computing has the potential to provide benefits to federal agencies; however, it can also create numerous information security risks. Since our report, federal agencies have taken several steps to address our recommendations on cloud computing security, but more remains to be done. For example, OMB has issued a cloud computing strategy; however the strategy does not fully address key information security challenges for agencies to adopt cloud computing. The CIO Council and GSA have also developed a shared assessment and authorization process, but this process has not yet been finalized. In addition, NIST has issued several publications addressing cloud computing security guidance. Although much has been done since our report, continued efforts will be needed to ensure that cloud computing is implemented securely in the federal government.

Organizations to Contact

The editors have compiled the following list of organizations concerned with the issues debated in this book. The descriptions are derived from materials provided by the organizations. All have publications or information available for interested readers. The list was compiled on the date of publication of the present volume; the information provided here may change. Be aware that many organizations take several weeks or longer to respond to inquiries, so allow as much time as possible.

Association for Computing Machinery (ACM)
2 Penn Plz., Suite 701, New York, NY   10121-0701
(800) 342-6626 • fax: (212) 944-1318
e-mail: acmhelp@acm.org
website: www.acm.org

As a membership organization comprised of computing professionals, the Association for Computing Machinery works to provide the computing community with the needed materials to advance the profession of computing science, further professional development, and support policy that improves society as a whole. With cloud computing becoming one of the hottest topics in society and the computing world, many ACM publications have focused on this technology. The ACM Queue website provides numerous articles on cloud computing, including "Cloud Computing: An Overview," "Why Cloud Computing Will Never Be Free," and "Securing Elasticity in the Cloud."

Center for Democracy and Technology (CDT)
1634 I St. NW, #1100, Washington, DC   20006
(202) 637-9800 • fax: (202) 637-0968
website: www.cdt.org

The Center for Democracy and Technology has worked since the early days of the Internet to ensure that policy and court decisions regarding this technology preserve freedom of ex-

pression, access, and privacy for all users. As Internet technologies have continued to develop, this organization has
strived to continually inform policymakers about necessary
changes to existing legislation. With regard to new cloud computing technology, CDT experts have testified that the Electronic Communications Privacy Act must be updated to ensure the protection of user privacy. Information about this
view and others relating to the cloud can be found on the
CDT website.

Computing Research Association (CRA)
1828 L St. NW, Suite 800, Washington, DC   20036-4632
(202) 234-2111 • fax: (202) 667-1066
e-mail: info@cra.org
website: www.cra.org

The Computing Research Association is a nonprofit membership organization that connects organizations from a variety
of backgrounds with the goal of improving computer focused
research and education. To achieve this goal, the association
focuses on four areas—policy influencing research, information collection and dissemination, professional computer technology community cohesion, and human resources development. As cloud computing has become more prominent in
the computer industry, CRA has increasingly focused on this
issue by publishing reports about its technical development,
with copies of these publications accessible on the
organization's website.

Distributed Computing Industry Association (DCIA)
2838 Cox Neck Rd., Suite 200, Chester, MD   21619
(410) 476-7965
e-mail: info@dcia.info
website: www.dcia.info

The Distributed Computing Industry Association provides a
central organizing body for members to join and address the
issues related to the development of the cloud computing industry. The DCIA site provides information about current ad-

vances in cloud computing standards, technology, and industry. Congressional testimony from DCIA officers regarding the growth, security, and privacy of cloud computing can be read on the site as well.

Electronic Frontier Foundation (EFF)
454 Shotwell St., San Francisco, CA   94110
(415) 436-9333 • fax: (415) 436-9993
e-mail: info@eff.org
website: www.eff.org

Since it was founded in 1990, the Electronic Frontier Foundation has fought to protect the free speech, privacy, innovation, and consumer rights of all individuals using the Internet. The organization faces both private companies and the US government in the courts to fight for the observance and preservation of these rights and mobilizes grassroots action to involve individuals in this fight. The EFF website provides access to a wide range of articles discussing these issues in relation to cloud computing, including "Is Cloud Computing Inherently Evil?" "How Safe Is Cloud Computing," and "Partly Cloudy Skies: Apple's Cloud Services Are Promising, But We Still Want a Freedom of Choice Button."

Electronic Privacy Information Center (EPIC)
1718 Connecticut Ave. NW, Suite 200, Washington, DC   20009
(202) 483-1140 • fax: (202) 483-1248
website: www.epic.org

The Electronic Privacy Information Center is a public interest research organization that focuses on protecting civil liberties and privacy, the First Amendment, and constitutional values in the face of emerging information technologies. Topics of interest include cloud computing, Facebook, Google Street View, and medical record privacy among others. With regard to cloud computing, EPIC emphasizes the need for stringent privacy protection methods to ensure the security of remotely stored user files. Details about this stance along with detailed case studies about individual sites and links to cloud news and resources are available on the EPIC website.

Institute for Ethics and Emerging Technologies (IEET)
Williams 119, Trinity College, 300 Summit St.
Hartford, CT   06106
(860) 297-2376
e-mail: director@ieet.org
website: www.ieet.org

The Institute for Ethics and Emerging Technologies seeks to bring public attention to the critical debates surrounding the ethical use of emerging technologies. Deeming itself a "technoprogressive" organization, IEET believes that positive human development can result from technological progress if the technologies are safe and distributed equally, and the organization strives to promote these two conditions. Information relating to cloud computing, an emerging technology examined by the organization, can be found on the IEET website in the form of articles, such as "Cloud Computing: Threat or Menace?" "What Are Mindfiles?" and more generally under topics such as Futurism, SciTech, and Privacy.

Institute of Electrical and Electronics Engineers (IEEE)
2001 L St. NW, Suite 700, Washington, DC   20036-4910
(202) 785-0017 • fax: (202) 785-0835
e-mail: ieeeusa@ieee.org
website: www.ieee.org

The Institute of Electrical and Electronics Engineers is a professional membership organization that strives to advance technology in responsible ways that benefit people worldwide. The IEEE strategy combines the use of publication, conferences, technology standards, and professional and educational activities to promote a global community of technology users. IEEE created a cloud computing initiative to lead in the advancement of the cloud and create a foundation for protocol, functionality, and governance. IEEE's official publication *IEEE Spectrum* offers articles about numerous cloud-related issues, including "Cloud Computing: It's Always Sunny in the Cloud" and "Your Security? Not Our Problem, Say Cloud Providers," all of which can be accessed online.

International Society for Technology in Education (ISTE)
1710 Rhode Island Ave. NW, Suite 900
Washington, DC   20036
(866) 654-4777 • fax: (202) 861-0888
e-mail: iste@iste.org
website: www.iste.org

The International Society for Technology in Education promotes innovative and effective uses of technology as a means to improve learning and teaching. Educators and education leaders can join this membership organization and collaborate with others to advance the use of technology in education. While the focus of the organization is broad with regard to technology use, cloud computing has become a focus within education, and as a result, ISTE has published many articles, including "Computing in the Clouds," "Cloud Computing? A Digital Equity Solution? Private Cloud for Educators? Tools for Kids as Netbooks?" and "Connected Classroom: A Personal Micro Database in the Cloud" to explore the ways in which cloud computing can be used to enhance education. These and others can be read on ISTE's website.

National Institute of Standards and Technology (NIST)
100 Bureau Dr., Stop 1070, Gaithersburg, MD   20899-1070
(301) 975-6478
e-mail: inquiries@nist.gov
website: www.nist.gov

The National Institute of Standards and Technology is a national, physical science laboratory dedicated to researching all technologies, from the smallest nanotechnology to the largest, man-made creations on the planet today. It seeks to utilize the findings of this research to encourage US innovation and help make America more competitive in the global world. One recent area of focus has been cloud computing and the ways in which this new technology can improve accessibility of information and reduce businesses' operating costs while maintaining high levels of security. Detailed information about cloud computing and the NIST efforts related to this technology can be found on the NIST website.

TechAmerica Foundation

601 Pennsylvania Ave. NW, North Building, Suite 600
Washington, DC 20004
(202) 682-9110 • fax: (202) 682-9111
website: www.techamericafoundation.org

The TechAmerica Foundation educates executives, policymakers, the press, opinion leaders, and the public on all facets of the technology industry in an effort to promote innovative technology ideas that have the potential to improve US economic growth and competitiveness. It does this through its publication of reports on the tech industry and economy, such as *Cyberstates, Cybercities,* and *Trade in the Cyberstates,* and reports aimed at explaining pertinent issues to the public in the *Competitiveness Series.* The foundation also provides guidance to the federal government regarding the implementation of cloud computing at the government level with the Commission on the Leadership Opportunity in the US Deployment of the Cloud. Information from this commission can be read online along with material about other cloud and computing issues.

Bibliography

Books

Lori B. Andrews   *I Know Who You Are and I Saw What You Did: Social Networks and the Death of Privacy.* New York: Free Press, 2012.

Nick Antonopoulos and Lee Gillam, eds.   *Cloud Computing: Principles, Systems, and Applications.* London, United Kingdom: Springer, 2010.

Charles Babcock   *Management Strategies for the Cloud Revolution: How Cloud Computing Is Transforming Business and Why You Can't Be Left Behind.* New York: McGraw-Hill, 2010.

Marc R. Benioff   *Behind the Cloud: The Untold Story of How Salesforce.com Went from Idea to Billion-Dollar Company—And Revolutionized an Industry.* San Francisco, CA: Jossey-Bass, 2009.

Rajkumar Buyya, James Broberg, and Andrzej Goscinkski, eds.   *Cloud Computing: Principles and Paradigms.* Hoboken, NJ: Wiley & Sons, 2011.

Nicholas G. Carr   *The Big Switch: Rewiring the World, from Edison to Google.* New York: Norton, 2008.

Peter Fingar   *Dot.cloud: The 21st Century Business Platform Built on Cloud Computing.* Tampa, FL: Meghan-Kiffer, 2009.

Michael H. Hugos and Derek Hulitzky — *Business in the Cloud: What Every Business Needs to Know About Cloud Computing.* Hoboken, NJ: Wiley & Sons, 2011.

Ronald L. Krutz and Russell Dean Vines — *Cloud Security: A Comprehensive Guide to Secure Cloud Computing.* Hoboken, NJ: Wiley & Sons, 2010.

Michael Miller — *Cloud Computing: Web-Based Applications That Change the Way You Work and Collaborate Online.* Indianapolis, IN: Que, 2009.

Evgeny Morozov — *The Net Delusion: The Dark Side of Internet Freedom.* New York: PublicAffairs, 2011.

Helen Fay Nissenbaum — *Privacy in Context: Technology, Policy, and the Integrity of Social Life.* Stanford, CA: Stanford Law, 2010.

Eli Pariser — *The Filter Bubble: What the Internet Is Hiding from You.* New York: Penguin, 2011.

Jothy Rosenberg and Arthur Mateos — *The Cloud at Your Service: The When, How, and Why of Enterprise Cloud Computing.* Greenwich, CT: Manning, 2011.

Daniel J. Solove — *Nothing to Hide: The False Tradeoff Between Privacy and Security.* New Haven, CT: Yale UP, 2011.

Barrie A. Sosinsky — *Cloud Computing Bible.* Indianapolis, IN: Wiley, 2011.

Lizhe Wang, Rajiv Ranjan, Jinjun Chen, and Boualem Benatallah, eds.   *Cloud Computing: Methodology, Systems, and Applications.* Boca Raton, FL: CRC, 2012.

Periodicals and Internet Sources

Jacob Aron   "Beware of the Botcloud," *New Scientist*, June 18, 2011. www.newscientist.com.

Kristen Berg   "Federal Government Enters the Era of the 'Cloud,'" *News Media & the Law*, Fall 2011.

Nick DeSantis   "Adrian Sannier Is Moving Classrooms to the Cloud," *Chronicle of Higher Education*, March 2, 2012.

Rik Fairlie   "Why You'll Love the Cloud," *Money*, September 2011.

James Fallows   "Hacked!" *Atlantic Monthly*, November 2011. www.theatlantic.com.

Geoffrey A. Fowler, Devlin Barret, Lucy Craymer, and Sam Schechner   "Megaupload Case Causes Ripple Effect," *Wall Street Journal*, January 25, 2012.

Simson L. Garfinkel   "The Cloud Imperative," *Technology Review*, November/December 2011.

Lev Grossman   "Cloud Control," *Time*, June 20, 2011. www.time.com.

Michael Healey   "Leap of Cloud Faith,"
InformationWeek, February 6, 2012.

Steve Knopper   "The Music Biz Bounces Back?"
Rolling Stone, December 22, 2011.

Robert L. Mitchell   "Integration in the Cloud,"
Computerworld, March 12, 2012.

Adam Mitton   "Trust Issues," *Lawyer*, October 31,
2011.

Eva Olasker   "Making Sense of Cloud Computing
in the Public Sector," *Government
Finance Review*, October 2011.

Steven
Rosenbaum   "Curate the Cloud," *EContent*,
December 2011.

Barry Sonnenfeld   "About This 'Cloud,'" *Esquire*,
October 2011.

S.J.
Vaughan-Nichols   "Operating Systems Don't Matter
Much Anymore," *Computerworld*,
December 5, 2011.

Art Wittmann   "Cloud Computing Still in Its
Adolescence," *InformationWeek*,
February 27, 2012.

Stewart Wolpin   "Burning Up the Web," *Popular
Science*, January 2012.
www.popsci.com.

Index

A

Amazon Kindle, 22–23, 47, 48, 50
Amazon server
    cloud computing and, 11, 35, 64
    EC2 cloud of, 37, 55
    movies from, 49
    security incidents, 97
Anderson, Mike, 38
Animal Farm (Orwell), 23
Apple
    cloud computing and, 21, 64
    iCloud service, 47, 50
    server utilization by, 67
Application programming interface (API), 13, 17
Armed Forces Communications and Electronics Association Cyber Committee, 40–46
Ars Technica, 31
Asia, 55, 56
Authority to Operate (ATO), 92
Automation concerns, 59–60

B

Blog sites, 24, 32–33
    See also individual blogs
Blossom, John, 75–76, 78–79
Botnets, 37
Brant, Ken, 58, 59
Broberg, James, 10–19
Brookings Institution, 73
Bryan, David, 34, 36, 37–38
Bush, George W., 27
Buyya, Rajkumar, 10–19

C

Center for Economics and Business Research, 55
Certification and Accreditation (C&A) process, 90
Chief information officers (CIOs), 87, 94, 102–103, 105–107
Christensen, Clay, 59
CIO Magazine, 8
Cisco Systems, 36
Client devices, 45–46
Client-server model, 63, 64
Climate change, 70, 72
Climate Group, 67
Clippinger, John, 77
Closed-web ecosystems, 31
Cloud computing
    community cloud, 99, 101
    defined, 7–9, 11–12, 26–27
    features of, 18–19
    hacking as threat, 34–39
    hardware virtualization, 15–17
    hybrid cloud, 99
    infiltrating, 35–36
    layers and types, 17–18
    onsite to remote service providers, 13–15
    overview, 10–19
    ownership issues and, 47–52
    pay-per-use services, 11–13
    private clouds, 59, 66, 99, 101
    security threats and, 40–46
    solutions to problems of, 30–31
    storage services, 7
    as user freedom threat, 20–28

O

P

R

S